Essential Personal Finance

There is increasing pressure for all of us to take responsibility for our own financial security and well-being, but we often overlook how the benefits that come with a job can help us do that. *Essential Personal Finance: A Practical Guide for Employees* focuses on these valuable work benefits and shows how you can build on this important foundation to achieve financial security and your life goals.

This unique book explores how making effective and practical use of these work benefits (such as pension scheme, life cover, sick pay, cheap loans, savings schemes and even financial coaching), means facing up to the behavioural biases we are all plagued with. Given that these can get in the way of even the best intentions, *Essential Personal Finance* tackles these biases head-on with practical ideas and tips for overcoming or harnessing them for good, and will help you to develop a positive and fruitful relationship with your money. With financial stress being a major cause of absenteeism and sick leave, low morale and lost productivity, the advice in this book also offers employers enormous benefits. By empowering employees through financial education and financial awareness, progressive employers will help them feel more in control of their lives, and experience less stress, resulting in higher morale and productivity.

Offering a distinctive approach which combines academic insight with practical financial wisdom and tools, this is a must-have book for all employees. It will help you make the most of everything your job has to offer so you can worry less about money and live life to the full.

Jonquil Lowe is Senior Lecturer in Economics and Personal Finance at The Open University, UK, and is also an independent practitioner who has published extensively on all aspects of personal finance. She started her working life in stockbroking but switched to consumer advocacy, becoming Head of Money Research at Which?, before launching her own freelance business.

Jason Butler is a Chartered Fellow of both the Chartered Institute for Securities & Investment and The Personal Finance Society. Following a 25-year career as a personal financial adviser, Jason is now Head of Financial Education at www.salaryfinance.com. He is also a personal finance columnist for *The Financial Times* and provides personal finance insights for Sky, BBC and a range of other media.

Lien Luu is a Chartered Fellow of the Personal Finance Society (part of the Chartered Institute of Insurance) and a Registered Life Planner with the Kinder Institute. Following many years as a financial planner, she is now an Associate Head of School at Coventry Business School, UK, where she enjoys lecturing on wealth management and writing books on personal finance.

Essential Personal Finance

A Practical Guide for Employees

Jonquil Lowe, Jason Butler and Lien Luu

Routledge
Taylor & Francis Group

LONDON AND NEW YORK

First published 2019
by Routledge
2 Park Square, Milton Park, Abingdon, Oxon OX14 4RN

and by Routledge
52 Vanderbilt Avenue, New York, NY 10017

Routledge is an imprint of the Taylor & Francis Group, an informa business

British Library Cataloguing-in-Publication Data
A catalogue record for this book is available from the British Library

Library of Congress Cataloging-in-Publication Data
Names: Lowe, Jonquil, author. | Luu, Liãen, 1967– author. | Butler, Jason
    (Financial planner), author.
Title: Essential personal finance : a practical guide for employees /
    Jonquil Lowe, Lien Luu and Jason Butler.
Description: Abingdon, Oxon ; New York, NY : Routledge, 2019. |
    Includes bibliographical references and index.
Identifiers: LCCN 2018038177 (print) | LCCN 2018047396 (ebook) |
    ISBN 9781351041669 (Ebook) | ISBN 9781138488113 (hardback : alk. paper) |
    ISBN 9781138488151 (pbk. : alk. paper) | ISBN 9781351041669 (ebk)
Subjects: LCSH: Employees—Finance, Personal.
Classification: LCC HG179 (ebook) | LCC HG179 .L588 2019 (print) |
    DDC 332.024—dc23
LC record available at https://lccn.loc.gov/2018038177

ISBN: 978-1-138-48811-3 (hbk)
ISBN: 978-1-138-48815-1 (pbk)
ISBN: 978-1-351-04166-9 (ebk)

Typeset in Optima
by Apex CoVantage, LLC

Printed and bound in Great Britain by
TJ International Ltd, Padstow, Cornwall

Contents

Figures

Tables

Introduction

It's hard to work effectively when you're worrying about money. A third of UK employees say financial worries are their biggest concern – ahead of health or work–life balance and way more significant than career development and workload. One in five say lost sleep due to financial worries reduces their ability to do their job. And workers struggling with money take more than twice as many days off sick as those without financial worries. It's estimated that employees' financial stress adds 4% to employers' costs (Barclays, 2014) in lost productivity and days off. So you and your employer both have strong reasons to care about your financial health and make it better.

Wages and salaries are the engine that pays the bills and allows you to plan ahead. But your workplace typically provides much more

  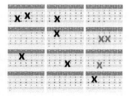

| For 1 in 3 money worries are the biggest concern | For 1 in 5 sleep lost worrying about money impairs work | 7 instead of 3 days a year lost if struggling with money |

Figure 0.1 How money worries affect employees' work

Sources: Neyber (2017); CIPD (2017); Willis Towers Watson (2016)

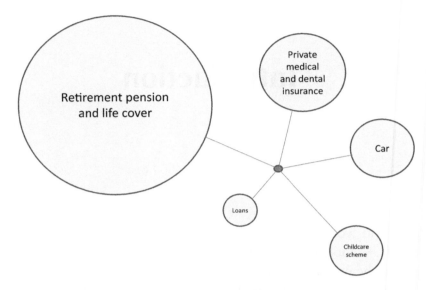

Figure 0.2 Common non-pay benefits from your workplace

Source: Author's chart. The relative size of the circles very loosely indicates how common each benefit is, based on data from HMRC (2018), ONS (2018) and Family and Childcare Trust (2016).

financial support than just pay. Some of the most common add-ons to your pay packet (benefits in kind) are shown in Figure 0.2. By far and away most widespread is a **pension scheme** that helps you build up an income for your eventual retirement. These schemes usually also provide **life cover** and **pensions** in the event of permanent ill-health or death, helping your family to be more financially secure. Some employers also offer help to you and your family with more transient health problems by arranging medical and dental **insurance**. Workplace benefits may also help you with costs like childcare and travel, for example through a company car or season-ticket loan. Some workplaces also give you access to **savings** schemes, such as a **credit union** or automated payments into an **individual savings account (ISA)**.

But, increasingly, enlightened employers are going beyond just providing financial products and are looking at how they can support you in the *process* of making good financial decisions. They are doing this by introducing financial workshops and coaching, available through the workplace. Like this book, their aim is to aid and support you as you navigate challenging issues like borrowing and managing debt, and building your financial security today and for tomorrow, and to put you on a path to achieve your goals whatever they may be.

The key to this approach is an understanding that money should promote, not interfere with, your happiness and ability to fulfil all that you do in work and life. In that spirit, the chapters that follow are a blueprint for taking control of your financial well-being, building on the resources that your earnings and workplace provide.

At their first mention, some terms are **highlighted like this** to indicate that you will find a definition in the *Glossary* at the back of the book.

An asterisk (*) after the name of an organisation indicates that you can find contact details in the *Useful contacts* section at the back of the book.

References

Barclays (2014) *Financial well-being: the last taboo in the workplace?* [online] https://wealth.barclays.com/content/dam/bwpublic/global/documents/global-stock-rewards/financial-well-being-report.pdf (accessed 15 June 2018).

Chartered Institute of Personnel Development (CIPD) (2017) *Financial well-being: the employee view* [online] www.cipd.co.uk/Images/financial-well-being-employee-view-report_tcm18-17439.pdf (accessed 15 June 2018).

Family and Childcare Trust (2016) *2016 Childcare Survey* [online] www.familyandchildcaretrust.org/childcare-survey-2016-0 (accessed 3 March 2018).

HM Revenue & Customs (HMRC) (2018) *Benefits in Kind Statistics July2018*, Table 4.1 [online] www.gov.uk/government/collections/taxable-benefits-in-kind-and-expenses-payments-statistics (accessed 19 September 2018).

Neyber (2017) *The DNA of financial wellbeing* [online] www.neyber.co.uk/resources/dna2017 (accessed 15 June 2018).

Office for National Statistics (2018) *Guide to Annual Survey of Hours and Earnings (ASHE), Pension estimates* [online] www.ons.gov.uk/employmentandlabourmarket/peopleinwork/workplacepensions/datasets/annualsurveyofhoursandearningspensiontablespensiontype byagegroupandbygrossweeklyearningsbandsp1 (accessed 3 March 2018).

Willis Towers Watson (2016) *Money worries and the workplace – why they matter* [online] www.towerswatson.com/en-GB/Insights/IC-Types/Ad-hoc-Point-of-View/2016/02/Money-worries-and-the-workplace-why-they-matter (accessed 15 June 2018).

Jobs, money and happiness

Jason Butler

In a nutshell:

- Developing a healthy relationship with money and understanding what is important to you in life are essential to making better financial decisions.
- Your job and how you use money play a big role in your financial well-being and happiness.
- There are simple ways to improve your happiness through better working, spending and saving decisions, habits and behaviours.

The role of money in your life

We all want to live a varied and long life that is as free from worry, stress and anxiety and as meaningful, enjoyable and comfortable as possible.

To survive and thrive we all need a certain amount of money to fund both the basics – food, shelter, energy, clothes and transport – and the extras that make life interesting and varied – entertainment, experiences and possessions. We also need to put aside money to support us when we can't or no longer want to work.

Most people need to sell their resources – time, energy, knowledge, skills and contacts – to generate the money to meet their basic and extra needs. As an employee you have chosen to sell your resources to an employer – whether in the public or private sector – in return for financial and non-financial rewards.

Your career and work choices, together with the daily financial decisions you make, will have a very big impact on your ability to live a life which is rich in every sense, and which enables you to be happy, secure and have choices.

The problem for most people is that money is an abstract concept and something with which most of us have a complicated and sometimes difficult relationship. Working out how money fits into your life, what makes you happy and what is truly important to you are the foundations of having a good relationship with money.

John Armstrong is a British psychologist who suggests four key questions to ask yourself about the role of money in your life. Take a few moments to think about your answers to each of his questions in Figure 1.1.

Developing the ability to understand what needs you are trying to meet and the role of money and work to meet those needs will help you to make better financial decisions. Understanding the impact of your spending on you and your life is crucial.

Armstrong suggests reducing our attachment to status and glamour in order to concentrate on higher, more meaningful things. This doesn't always require more money but presence of mind and self-control plus a healthy relationship with money.

Financial well-being

Human well-being comprises five elements (Rath and Harter, 2010):

- **Career** (how you spend your time)
- **Social** (relationships and love)
- **Physical** (good health and energy)
- **Community** (engagement with where you live) and
- **Financial** (the amount of money you have and the way you use it).

The role of money in your life
1. What do I need money for? That is, what is important to me?
2. How much money do I need to do that?
3. What is the best way for me to get that money?
4. What are my economic responsibilities to other people?

Figure 1.1 The role of money in your life

Source: Adapted from: *How to Worry Less about Money* (Armstrong, 2012)

Financial well-being has been defined (CFPB, 2015) as follows:

Financial well-being can be defined as a state of being wherein a person can fully meet current and ongoing financial obligations, can feel secure in their financial future, and is able to make choices that allow enjoyment of life.

Financial well-being can also be broken down into four key components, which are shown in Figure 1.2.

There are several degrees of financial well-being or wellness, and these can be likened to a staircase as shown in Figure 1.3, together with the percentage of UK households in each category.

THE FOUR ELEMENTS OF FINANCIAL WELLBEING

Figure 1.2 The four elements of financial well-being

Source: Based on concepts set out in *Financial Well-being: The Goal of Financial Education*, Consumer Financial Protection Bureau, p.19

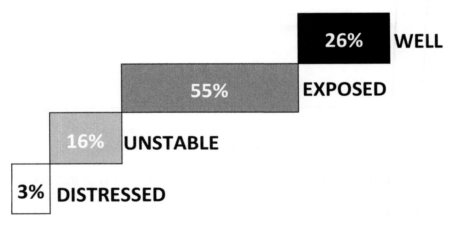

Figure 1.3 The financial wellness staircase

Source: Based on data from *Momentum UK Household Financial Wellness Index 2017 Summary Report.*

One way to maximise your own financial well-being is by gaining insights, understanding and awareness of the attitudes, habits and behaviours necessary to enable you to get the most daily happiness and long-term well-being from your money and work.

The role of work

Most research suggests that our genes and personality influence about 50% of how happy we feel, with the balance influenced by our health, employment and relationships.

The authors of the *World Happiness Report* (Helliwell et al., 2017) explained the importance of jobs and working to overall human well-being:

> The importance of having a job extends far beyond the salary attached to it, with non-pecuniary aspects of employment such as social status, social relations, daily structure, and goals all exerting a strong influence on people's happiness.

So, in addition to the obvious financial rewards, the non-financial aspects of a job and working are clearly very important. That's why people who are unemployed for more than a few months can experience real misery and unhappiness – they suffer much more than just a loss of income. Various studies (Clark, 2003; Dolan and White, 2008) show that unemployment has a strong and negative association with well-being, which is why arguably any job is better than no job, at least from a well-being perspective.

It's therefore no surprise that, despite wages falling in real terms over the five years to the end of 2017, with employment in the UK at record levels, official measurements of average life satisfaction, life feeling worthwhile and happiness ratings have reached their highest levels since 2011, as shown in Figure 1.4.

Mental and physical health

Maintaining purpose in life has been shown to be a be significant factor in overall well-being and how long one lives. For many people work gives them that purpose.

A study of people in their sixties in the US, UK and Europe found a strong link between early retirement and a reduction in mental capability – known as cognitive decline (Rohwedder and Willis,

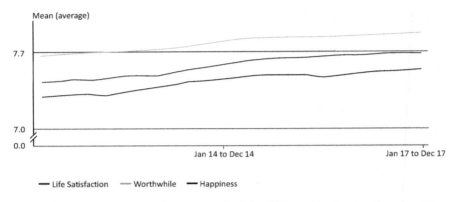

Figure 1.4 Average life satisfaction, worthwhile and happiness ratings, year ending March 2012 to year ending December 2017

Source: Office for National Statistics, 2018. Data from the annual population survey

Reg's story

Reg started work at 13 as a coal miner's assistant in South Wales in 1937. When the local mine closed Reg moved to Birmingham to work in various factories until they were bombed in the Second World War.

Reg then moved back to South Wales where he got a job as a fireman loading coal on a steam train. Some years later Reg progressed to driving trains, which he did until he was made redundant in 1964 when his depot closed.

Reg then re-invented himself as a machinist for industrial chemicals group ICI, where he trained others until he was made redundant in 1979 aged 56. Despite being unemployed for two years, Reg eventually got a job as a checkout operator at J Sainsbury's, the supermarket chain.

In 1988, when he reached age 65, Reg retired from Sainsbury's but after just six weeks he felt bored and asked for his old job back. When asked why he wasn't retired Reg said: 'You've got to stay active to stay alive. I love my job and want to keep doing it for as long as I can.'

Despite the death of his wife in 2011, Reg finally found love again when he met Ruth in 2014.

Reg stayed at Sainsbury's for a total of 29 years after his first 'retirement' until his 'final' retirement at age 94 in autumn 2017, which was seven years later than his son Michael's retirement in 2010.

2010). Another study of US adults concluded that there may be a link between early retirement and early death and improved lifespan from retiring later (Wu et al., 2016).

It might, therefore, make sense to plan on working longer, but perhaps less intensively as you get older. As well as the potential health benefits, this has the added benefit of giving you longer to save and a shorter retirement to fund.

Job fit

Some jobs appear to deliver more happiness and satisfaction than others. A 2012 survey of 2,200 UK workers found that gardeners and florists topped the list of happiest workers, followed by hairdressers and plumbers. Meanwhile, bankers, IT professionals and human resources workers were the least happy, as set out in Figure 1.5.

Another recent global study (Indeed, 2016) of job happiness found that work–life balance was the single most important factor affecting workers' happiness with their work.

The most important contributing factor to job happiness is the degree to which employees are able to find harmony between the demands of work and their personal lives.

	% AGREEING THEY ARE HAPPY	ATTRIBUTE THAT RESPONDENTS MOST ASSOCIATED WITH THEIR JOB
Florists & gardeners	87%	I am in a working environment that I like and I do something worthwhile and useful (89%)
Hairdressers & beauticians	79%	I have control of duties, manage my own workload and have stimulating work (71%)
Plumbers & water workers	76%	I get on well with colleagues (78%)
Marketers & PR	75%	I get on well with colleagues and I am in a working environment that I like (75%)
Scientists & researchers	69%	I get on well with colleagues (90%)
Leisure & tourism workers	67%	I get on well with colleagues (87%)
Construction workers	66%	I get on well with colleagues (81%)
Doctors & dentists	65%	I get on well with colleagues (88%)
Lawyers	64%	I get on well with colleagues (86%)
Nurses	62%	I feel that I am doing something worthwhile and useful (87%)
Architects	62%	I get on well with colleagues (81%)
Childcare & youth workers	60%	I feel that I am doing something worthwhile and useful (82%)
Teachers	59%	I get on well with colleagues (86%)
Accountants	58%	I get on well with colleagues (79%)
Car workers & mechanics	57%	I get on well with colleagues (86%)
Electricians	55%	I have control of duties, and manage my own workload (78%)
Caterers	55%	I get on well with colleagues (85%)
HR & personnel staff	54%	I have control of duties, and manage my own workload (79%)
IT & telecoms workers	48%	I get on well with colleagues (83%)
Bankers	44%	I get on well with colleagues (76%)

Figure 1.5 Career happiness index

Source: City & Guilds 2012. 13 November: https://www.cityandguilds.com/news/November-2012/careers-happiness-index-2012#.WmYarZOFiuU

Question: How important is your current job to your overall sense of happiness and well-being?

1	2	3	4	5	6	7	8	9	10
Not at all--Totally									

But what if you can't find a job that you love or that delivers the right work–life balance? It is certainly the case that many people, at least for some of their working life, must do jobs that are not ideal or don't make them happy. If this is the case for you, then there are two practical things you can do to improve your happiness:

1. Take pride in the daily work you do and the associated tasks. This will enable you, no matter how unglamorous or unpleasant the job might be, to 'win' every day and that will help improve your overall happiness. It also has the potential to help you get a job more suited to your strengths and preferences, because your attitude will mark you out as a good worker.
2. Seek happiness and fulfilment in the activities you do outside work, such as hobbies and pastimes that you enjoy. If you can do these activities with other people, even better, as human interaction is also a key element of personal happiness.

Financial rewards from working

Economic motivation

Most people have an economic motivation to work – they need to earn an income to meet their daily living costs.

Professor Michael Norton, of Harvard University, has carried out several studies into money and happiness, and he concludes that 'More money is never worse than having less money – because we still find that people with more money are happier. But how you use the money and how you think about money are critical' (Norton and Garcia-Rad, 2018).

13

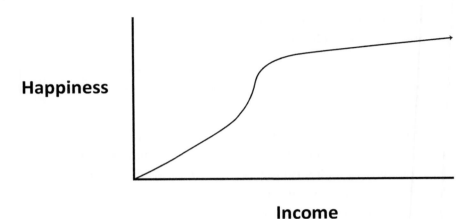

Happiness

Income

Figure 1.6 Income and happiness
Source: Author's diagram

But while not having enough income to meet your basic needs certainly leads to unhappiness, having more income than you need doesn't necessarily lead to ever greater happiness (Kahneman and Deaton, 2010; Jebb et al, 2018) as shown visually in Figure 1.6.

In effect the more you earn above a certain point (which will vary from person to person and country to country), the less happiness you get for each unit of earnings until further happiness gains are negligible.

Income and happiness are relative

Would you prefer to live in a world where:

- the average salary was £25,000 and you earned £50,000, or
- you earned £100,000 but the average salary was £200,000?

A version of this question was posed to US workers in the 1990s (Solnick and Hemenway, 1998). Nearly half of the respondents said they'd prefer to live in a world where the average salary was $25,000 and they earned $50,000 than one where they earned $100,000 but the average was $200,000.

It seems that we also care a lot about how much we earn compared to our peers and colleagues and that the effect increases as our income rises. We are happiest when we don't just have enough for our day-to-day needs, but we also earn more than people like us (Blanchflower and Oswald, 2004).

It has been found that we also derive happiness from continual and meaningful rises in income throughout our working lives (Di Tella and MacCulloch, 2010). So, undertaking training and development to improve your skills, capabilities and usefulness should be very positive for your overall well-being.

A recent survey of UK individuals found that how much spare income you have i.e. after meeting fixed and variable living costs each month, is linked to your level of happiness. The study found that the happiest 10% of households have £841 per month spare income – equivalent to £356 per person per month or £82 per week, as shown in Figure 1.7.

We don't know for sure whether happier people spend less and so have more surplus income or if having a higher surplus income makes them happier. Either way the average person in the UK has £44 per week spare cash, meaning that they would need to find just

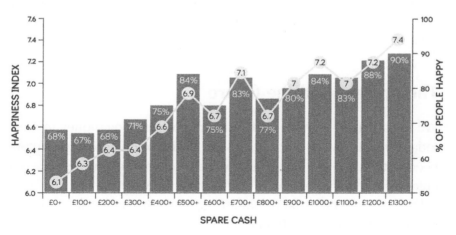

Figure 1.7 Spare cash v happiness

Source: *Cash Happy: The 2017 Annual Report*, Sun Life

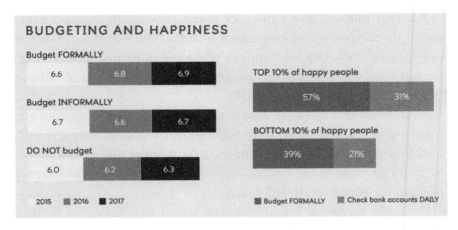

BUDGETING AND HAPPINESS

Figure 1.8 Budgeting and happiness

Note: The left-hand graphic shows a happiness rating out of 10 for each respondent category

Source: *Cash Happy: The 2017 Annual Report,* Sun Life

£5 a day to have a surplus income the same as the happiest 10% of people. That could be achieved by cutting out a takeaway coffee and sandwich or going out one night less each week.

Having a formal **budget** and keeping on top of your bank account may also improve your happiness. There is some evidence of a strong correlation between budgeting and happiness as shown in Figure 1.8.

We'll look at budgeting and ways of increasing spare cash in Chapter 2.

The present and the future

We are all faced with the daily dilemma of spending money to meet today's needs, wants and desires, or **saving** money to meet future needs. Studies show that, generally, we discount the future and favour enjoying and experiencing things in the here and now.

We have two financial personalities, which influence all our financial decisions. Richard Thaler and Cass Sunstein, two distinguished professors of behavioural economics, describe these personalities as a far-sighted 'planner' and a **myopic** 'doer'. The planner represents the reflective thinking mode and the doer represents the instinctive mode.

In their bestselling book *Nudge* (2009) Thaler and Sunstein explain the two financial personalities like this:

> The Planner is trying to promote your long-term welfare but must cope with the feelings, mischief, and strong will of the Doer, which is exposed to the temptations that come with arousal.
>
> Recent research in neuroeconomics has found evidence consistent with this two-system conception of self-control. Some parts of the brain get tempted, and other parts are prepared to enable us to resist temptation by assessing how we should react to the temptation.
>
> Sometimes the two parts of the brain can be in severe conflict – a kind of battle that one or the other is bound to lose.

When we spend money, we are always seeking to meet a need. Sometimes that need is obvious – hunger, thirst etc. In many cases that need is not obvious. For example, shopping for clothes when you

THE DOER

- SELF-INTEREST
- MYOPIC
- IMPULSIVE
- SHORT-SIGHTED

V

THE PLANNER

- BEST-INTERESTS
- RATIONAL
- REFLECTIVE
- FAR-SIGHTED

Figure 1.9 The two financial personalities

Source: Author's diagram

already have plenty of suitable things to wear might relate to a need to be accepted by others, help you bolster your self-esteem or relieve boredom.

Every spending decision is to meet a need. The question is could you meet that need without spending money or at the very least by spending less? Developing this awareness and self-control is essential to money being a force for good in your life.

Sally's story

Sally is in her late 20s, single and in a well-paid job. She regularly goes overdrawn, although she always repays her substantial **credit card** balance in full each month.

Sally has no savings. Her weakness is shoes, on which it is common for her to spend £150 per month. She has about 60 pairs of shoes and is embarrassed that she has never worn some pairs and others only a few times.

Clearly Sally doesn't *need* all these shoes to wear but buying them is meeting another deep-seated need. Unless she identifies this need and devises another way of meeting it which doesn't involve spending money, or at least much less than she currently does, she will continue to be unable to build any savings while continuing to accumulate more unused pairs of shoes.

Question: Think about a recent time when you bought something that you didn't strictly need.

What motivated you to buy it? _____

What emotion did you feel immediately after the purchase?

_____

Is the purchase still making you feel that same emotion now?

_____

What real need do you think you were trying to meet with the purchase? _____

How could you meet that need without spending?

_____

If you don't curtail your doer's instinctive bias for the present, your daily spending will be directed to things that give you immediate reward and pleasure. This will reduce your ability to build financial resilience, freedom of choice and security in the **long term**.

How to control your spending impulses

There are several ways to reduce your doer's influence on your daily spending.

Commit to a financial goal

For example, you might want to buy a house in three years and need to have saved a £20,000 deposit. If you have no savings to start with you will need to save about £540 per month if **interest** is 2% per annum.

Knowing that impulsive spending might eat into your monthly saving and therefore stop you being able to buy the house could help you resist the urge to spend.

Sharing the goal with a friend and agreeing some form of sanction if you don't stick to your savings program might also help you stay disciplined.

Labelling the account with the goal you are saving for such as 'House deposit fund' might also help you stay the course.

Take a few minutes to jot down your key financial goals, when you want to have reached them and the amount (if known).

Your key financial goals		
Goal	By when?	How much?

Avoid comparing yourself to other people

There will always be someone with more and better things than you and their idea of what matters is unlikely to be the same as yours. Facebook and Instagram are awash with people seemingly having a better life than you, with more friends, more holidays, better clothes, more beauty and more fun.

Spending your money to impress other people isn't just a loser's game, it also helps to keep you poor and reduces your financial resilience, future life choices and security. And there is a substantial body of research which suggests comparing yourself to others and buying 'stuff' has a seriously negative impact on your happiness (Frank, 2004; Solnick and Hemenway, 1998; Van Boven et al., 2010).

In her 2009 biography of Will Smith, Lisa Lannucci quotes the actor Will Smith as saying his favourite quote is:

> Too many people spend money they haven't earned, to buy things they don't want, to impress people they don't like.

Question: Imagine you were the only person in the world. Assume that you could cope with the loneliness and that everything still works (electricity, goods in shops etc.). Would you still wear the same clothes, use beauty products, drive the same car, wear jewellery, live in the same house?

Take a moment to note any recent spending which you've done to impress others, even if this was, on reflection, subconsciously.

Recent spending I've done to impress others		
Item	How much?	Still making me happy? Y/N

Don't shop when you are sad

You are more likely to make impulsive and unnecessary purchases when you feel down (Fenton-O'Creevy et al., 2018).

In fact, purchasing things when you are sad is also likely to reinforce the sadness that you are trying to alleviate, because anything you buy that's associated with whatever you're trying to forget just serves to remind you of that setback or failure. Instead of being a consolation prize it acts as a trigger that makes you feel even worse, chips away at your self-control and even impairs your ability to focus on completing difficult tasks (Lisjak et al., 2015), as the researcher explains:

> After experiencing a setback in one area of their life, consumers might be better off boosting their sense of self in a different area of their life.

Regularly look at a picture of the older you

Retirement, being a rather abstract and vague issue, *feels* so far away and there are so many things you could enjoy right now which are more tangible and vivid!

Psychologists call this situation **psychological distance**.

This can make it very hard to forgo spending on things that give immediate reward in order to save for your retirement or other long-term goals.

One way to reduce impulsive spending and make your future feel more real and important is to have a clear picture of your future self.

Research by Dr. Hal Hershfield (2010) shows that people who interacted with a detailed avatar of their future self made more patient financial decisions.

> Specifically, when the future self shares similarities with the present self, when it is viewed in vivid and realistic terms, and when it is seen in a positive light, people are more willing to make choices today that may benefit them at some point in the years to come.

One way to reduce the psychological distance between your present and future self is to use one of the many age-progression applications to create a vivid picture of how you might look in 20 or 30 years' time.

Aging apps (choose one that is free to download) work by taking a picture of you and digitally changing it to show what you might look like when you are in your 80s or 90s.

Dr Hershfield's research suggests that regularly checking in with your older self in this way can help reduce impulsive spending and increase long-term saving.

Create and work to a monthly budget

Working out where your money goes on fixed and variable regular expenses will enable you to develop a sense of how much money you can and want to let your doer spend on fun and impulsive things.

For example, you might have £300 per month surplus and agree that you can spend £100 per month (about £23 per week) on anything that takes your fancy, but if you spend £90 in the first week, that means there is nothing for the next three weeks.

See Chapter 2 for more on how to budget.

Avoid using contactless card payment

Contactless payment can increase both the amount and frequency of impulsive spending by as much as 30%, compared to paying for things with physical cash (Nunes and Boatwright, 2004).

Until you have developed good self-control and spending discipline, use cash as much as possible to pay for smaller purchases. The physical act of handing over coins and notes and seeing the money in your purse or wallet reduce will keep you more connected with your spending.

Take a breath and pause

Every time you are thinking of spending money say to yourself 'Do I really need this?'. Or you could just decide to defer the purchase to the following day. If you still want the item the next day then go ahead, but there is a good chance that you won't feel the same desire to spend.

Learning to say 'NO' more and 'YES' less to spending is a key habit to cultivate.

Roger and Lara's story

Roger and Lara thought their dream had come true when they won £1.8m in the National Lottery in 2005. The well-educated, hard-working couple had been married for ten years and seemed to have it all.

Roger immediately quit his job as an IT manager and Lara gave up her job as a performing arts teacher. Roger spent thousands recording and promoting an album, while Lara bought a beauty salon.

They swapped their ex-council house for a large barn conversion and both bought expensive cars. Roger tried his hand at small-scale property developments. They enjoyed numerous expensive foreign holidays and nights out to high-end restaurants. Roger and Lara's children were sent to expensive private schools.

But eventually the good times came to an end.

A massive fire at their home required them to live in temporary accommodation.

Eight years later Roger had just £7 in the bank, Lara was having to work all hours in the beauty salon she used to own, the bank was about to repossess their home and their marriage was in tatters.

Overspending on lavish holidays, expensive cars and designer handbags, bad **investments**, ill-judged business ventures and Roger stopping work to pursue his dream of being a rock star, all contributed to their downfall.

Actions

List the specific actions you will take NOW to help control your spending. I've given you an example for the first one.

Controlling spending	
Tactic	Specific action
Payment method	Cut up all but one existing credit card and keep the remaining one in a drawer at home.

The power of self-belief

Research suggests that the more positive your beliefs and attitudes about money; the more you believe that good money behaviour is what others expect of you (the social norm); the more you have belief in your ability to adopt positive money behaviours, the better you'll be with money; and as a result, you'll be happier (Ajzen, 1991). Or as Henry Ford is reported to have said 'If you think you can, you're right.'

More recent research (Morningstar, 2017) supporting this theory found that people who agreed with the statement 'I create my own financial destiny', and therefore are taking responsibility for their financial future, have a better relationship with and attitude towards money.

> Across all income levels, people who believe they create their own financial destiny experience, on average, more positive emotions with respect to money, than those who believe they have less power.
>
> The lesson here is fascinating: A sense of personal power – not money itself – may be the key to emotional well-being in our financial lives.

Those who feel more empowered and in control of their finances experience much better emotional well-being and much less stress and anxiety as shown in the chart Figure 1.10.

Conclusion

The writer Francis Bacon wrote in the 1600s that 'Money is a good servant, a bad master'. Learning to master your own money is key to leading a fulfilling life and minimising stress and worry.

Understanding the role of money in your life, spending on things that deliver lasting happiness, saving enough surplus income for when you can't or no longer wish to work, and being prepared for setbacks and challenges are all essential elements to maximising your financial well-being.

Emotional well-being by income and empowerment

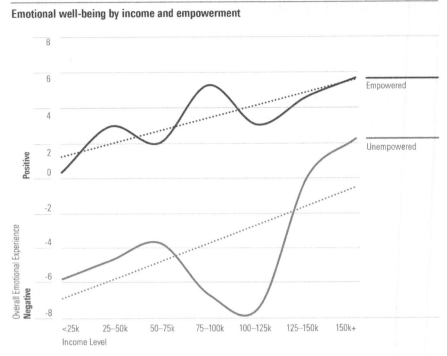

Figure 1.10 Emotional well-being by empowerment

In the next chapter we discuss how to develop the context to ensure that you make smart decisions about working, spending and saving, so that money supports the life you want and deserve.

Note

1   © 2017 Morningstar, Inc. All Rights Reserved. The information contained herein: (1) is proprietary to Morningstar and/or its content providers; (2) may not be copied or distributed; (3) does not constitute investment advice offered by Morningstar; and (4) is not warranted to be accurate, complete or timely. Neither Morningstar nor its content providers are responsible for any damages or losses arising from any use of this information. Past performance is no guarantee of future results. Use of information from Morningstar does not necessarily constitute agreement by Morningstar, Inc. of any investment philosophy or strategy presented in this publication.

References

Ajzen, I. (1991) 'The theory of planned behaviour'. *Organisational Behaviour and Human Decision Processes,* 50(2): 179–211.

Armstrong, J. 2012 *How to Worry Less about Money.* London: MacMillan.

Bacon, Francis (1623) *De Dignitate et Augmentis Scientiarum – Book Six.*

Blanchflower, David G. and Oswald, Andrew J. (2004) 'Well-being over time in Britain and USA'. *Journal of Public Economics,* 88(7): 1359–86.

City & Guilds (2012) *Career Happiness Index* [online] www.cityandguilds. com/news/November-2012/careers-happiness-index-2012#.WmYar-ZOFiuU (accessed 13 November 2017).

Clark, R.E. (2003) 'Fostering the work motivation of individuals and teams'. *Performance Improvement,* 42(3): 21–9 [online] http://projects.ict.usc. edu/itw/vtt/Clark_MotivationPI_03.pdf (accessed 24 January 2018).

Consumer Financial Protection Bureau (2015). *Financial Well-being: The Goal of Financial Education,* p.18 [online] http://files.consumerfinance. gov/f/201501_cfpb_report_financial-well-being.pdf (accessed 24 January 2018).

Di Tella, Rafael and MacCulloch, Robert J. (2010) 'Happiness adaptation to income beyond "basic needs" '. In Ed Diener, John F. Helliwell and Daniel Kahneman, eds, *International Differences in Well-being,* pp.139–65. Oxford: Oxford University Press.

Dolan, P., Peasgood, T. and White, M. (2008) 'Do we really know what makes us happy? A review of the economic literature associated with subjective well-being'. *Journal of Economic Psychology,* 29: 94–122.

Fenton-O'Creevy, M., Dibbs, S. and Furnham, A. (2018) 'Antecedents and consequences of chronic impulsive buying: can impulsive buying be understood as dysfunctional self regulation?' [online] http://oro.open. ac.uk/53395/8/P%26M-authors-version.pdf (accessed 31 May 2018).

Frank, R.H. (2004) 'How not to buy happiness'. *Daedalus,* 133: 69–79.

Helliwell, J., Layard, R. and Sachs, J., (2017) *World Happiness Report 2017,* New York: Sustainable Development Solutions Network, p.145 [online] https://s3.amazonaws.com/happiness-report/2017/HR17.pdf (accessed 24 January 2018).

Hershfield, H. (2010) 'Future self-continuity: how conceptions of the future self transform intertemporal choice'. *Annals of the New York Academy of Sciences,* 1235(1): 30–43.

The Indeed Job Happiness Index (2016) *Ranking the World for Employee Satisfaction* [online] http://blog.indeed.com/hiring-lab/indeed-job-happiness-index-2016/ (accessed 22 October 2017).

Jebb, A.T., Tay, L., Diener, E. and Shigehiro, O. (2018) 'Happiness, income satiation and turning points around the world'. *Nature Human Behaviour*, 2: 33–8.

Kahneman, D. and Deaton, A., (2010). 'High income improves evaluation of life but not emotional well-being'. *Proceedings of the National Academy of Sciences,* 107 (38): 16489–93.

Lannucci, L. (2009) *Will Smith: A Biography.* Greenwood.

Lisjak, M., Bonezzi, A., Kim, S. and Rucker, Derek D. (2015) 'Perils of compensatory consumption: within-domain compensation undermines subsequent self-regulation'. *Journal of Consumer Research*, 41(5): 1186–1203 [online] www.jstor.org/stable/10.1086/678902 (accessed 30 October 2017).

Momentum UK (2017) *Momentum UK Household Financial Wellness Index 2017 Summary Report* [online] www.momentumgim.co.uk/wps/wcm/connect/mgim2/3a6e04d0-4d20-47f9-b1e2-26ed81db67bb/Final+-summary+report+-+Financial+Wellness+2017.pdf?MOD=AJPERES (accessed 21 October 2017).

Morningstar (2017) 'When more is less: rethinking financial health' [online] http://images.mscomm.morningstar.com/Web/MorningstarInc/%7B-b87a29d4-9264-4e6f-a5d7-5e65f8714f92%7D_US_ADV_MoreLess_Whitepaper_Final.pdf (accessed 22 April 2018).

Norton, M. and Garcia-Rad, X. (2018) *How Happy Relationships Relate to Money* [online] www.ezonomics.com/stories/how-happy-relationships-relate-to-money/ (accessed 2 March 2018).

Nunes, J.C. and Boatwright, P. (2004) 'Incidental prices and their effect on willingness to pay'. *Journal of Marketing Research*, XLI: 457–66.

Office for National Statistics (2018) Personal well-being in the UK: January to December 2017 [online] www.ons.gov.uk/peoplepopulationandcommunity/wellbeing/bulletins/measuringnationalwellbeing/januaryto-december2017 (accessed 31 May 2018).

Rohwedder, S. and Willis, R.J. (2010) 'Mental Retirement'. *Journal of Economic Perspectives*, 24(1): 119–38.

Rath, T. and Harter, J. (2010) *Wellbeing: The Five Essential Elements.* Gallup Press.

Solnick, Sara J. and Hemenway, D. (1998) 'Is more always better?' *Journal of Economic Behavior & Organization*, Nov. [online] www.dl.icdst.org/pdfs/files/64d27b6bd5694361593729862f6a35bf.pdf (accessed 24 January 2018).

Sun Life (2017) *Cash Happy: The 2017 Annual Report* [online] www.sunlife.co.uk/siteassets/documents/cash-happy/cash-happy-report-2017.pdf (accessed 20 January 2018).

Thaler, R. and Sunstein, C. (2009) *Nudge*, pp.45–6. London: Penguin Books.

Van Boven, L., Campbell, M.C. and Gilovich, T. (2010) 'Stigmatizing materialism: on stereotypes and impressions of materialistic and experiential pursuits'. *Personality and Social Psychology Bulletin*, 36: 551–63.

Wu, C., Odden, M.C., Fisher, G.G. *et al.* (2016) 'Association of retirement age with mortality: a population-based longitudinal study among older adults in the USA'. *J. Epidemiol Community Health*, 70: 917–23 [online] http://jech.bmj.com/content/70/9/917 (accessed 15 January 2018).

2 | Work and financial planning

Jason Butler

In a nutshell:

- **Human capital is the source of all financial capital.**
- **Financial planning helps improve well-being.**
- **Understand basic financial planning principles and practices.**

Human capital: the foundation of wealth creation

Your ability to earn money throughout your life is a tremendous asset. The total value (today) of all future earnings throughout your working life is known as **human capital**.

A very important concept to understand is that your human capital comes from your individual resources – time, energy, knowledge, skills, reputation – which can be leased to an employer for a monthly fee in the form of your salary or wages.

Each month you convert some of your human capital into a cash inflow. You then have a choice between spending it now or saving it in the form of **assets**. These may be **financial capital** (investments, pensions, property and **physical assets**) to spend at a later date, typically when you can't or don't wish to work.

Your human capital is likely to be your largest asset and your financial capital represents the proportion of your human capital that you have chosen to defer to spend later. This is shown graphically in Figure 2.1.

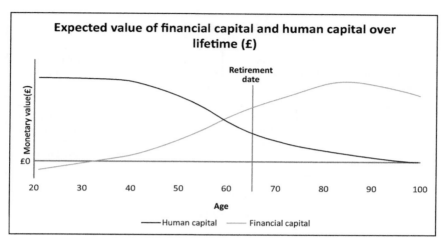

Figure 2.1 Human and financial capital over lifetime
Source: Authors' chart

What you spend today means converting less of your human capital into financial capital (including physical assets, such as housing). As you age, and your remaining years of paid work reduce, your human capital reduces.

Weighing up whether to consume your income today or defer spending by saving some of your income is the classic trade-off that we all have to make as we go through life.

As I discussed in Chapter 1, in the real world we all have to find the right balance between using money to enjoy things now and deferring consumption and saving for longer-term goals such as **financial independence**.

Save too little and the chances are you'll end up either working until you drop or being poor in older age. Save too much and you'll possibly not enjoy life as much as you might otherwise have (or have worked too hard to earn money), with the possibility that you die or become seriously ill before you manage to enjoy the fruits of your labour.

A point that comes up a lot with younger audiences I speak to about financial well-being, is their concern that automation and **artificial**

The four planning principles of human capital	
You need to convert some of your human capital into financial capital as you progress through your working life	To create financial capital you need to earn more than you spend each year and save and invest the difference
Investing in your skills and capabilities and gaining experience can increase your human capital by increasing future earnings potential	You need to maintain good mental and physical health to preserve your human capital and have adequate insurance to protect against the financial impact of ill health or early death

Figure 2.2 Four principles of human capital

Source: Author's categorisation

intelligence may take their job and affect their earning potential (and in turn the value of their human capital).

The world of work is continually changing and adapting, new needs are being found and new products and services are, and will continue to be, developed to meet those needs. While some human jobs will be eradicated, many other new roles will be created.

It is against this backdrop of a continually changing world of work, that you need to continually invest in improving your human capital. You do this by improving your skills, knowledge, capability, adaptability and usefulness, through both on the job experience, formal training and qualifications and pushing yourself to do things that are outside of your 'comfort zone'.

Investing time and money in your human capital is likely to be the best investment you can ever make, particularly if you are aged below 45, because it will enable you to stay in demand from employers or customers as technology changes the employment landscape and increase how much you earn over your lifetime.

Many employers now offer a range of training and personal development opportunities, whether in terms of giving you time off, financial assistance or in-house schemes, so investigate what is available at your company.

As you can see from the chart in Figure 2.3, investing a few thousand pounds to improve skills to increase annual salary rises from 3%

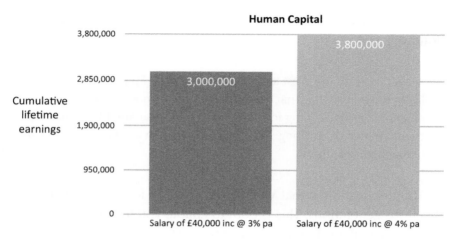

Figure 2.3 Cumulative value of human capital for a 25-year-old with a
40-year career

Source: Author's diagram

to 4% per annum is far more valuable in human capital terms than any other investment is likely to return.

Particularly if you are young, it is far better for your overall financial position to achieve an extra 1% annual salary growth – thereby increasing the **present value** of your human capital – than having a £1,000 raise that only rises at 3% per annum in the future or getting 1% per annum extra **investment returns** on your financial capital.

A long life: staying young for longer

Unless you've been holed up on a desert island for the past 20 years, you'll be aware that we are all living longer as a result of better medical care, rising living standards and the eradication of many manual and strenuous jobs.

But few people realise just how long they are likely to live, which has massive implications for working, spending and saving decisions.

In their thought-provoking book, *The 100-year Life: Living and Working in an Age of Longevity*, eminent London Business School professors Lynda Gratton and Andrew Scott set out the stark facts as follows:

> A child born in the West today has more than a 50 percent chance of living to be over 105. That means that if you are now 20 you have a 50 percent chance of living to more than 100; if you are 40 you have an evens chance of reaching 95; if you are 60, then a 50 percent chance of making 90 or more.

The implication is that you'll need to work for much longer than previous generations. This is both to enable you to accumulate sufficient financial assets to live off when you stop earning an income and to defer the date from which you'll need to draw upon that capital to fund your lifestyle.

Gratton and Scott suggest that while the traditional three stage life of education, career and retirement might still be within reach of a significant number of people over 45, for many others, including most young people, it unlikely to be financially feasible. But aside from the financial imperative of working longer, there is also the important point that it is likely to be good for your mental and physical health.

Developing and maintaining a longer-term financial plan and making wise day-to-day financial decisions is essential if you want to be able to live a long and fulfilled life without money worries or troubles.

What is financial planning?

If you were going to build a house, you'd clearly need to do a fair bit of preparation beforehand. You'd need to work out where and what you'd like to build. You'd get an architect to draw up some plans, and you'd have to obtain planning permission from the local authority.

Then you'd need to get quotes for labour and materials, choose a contractor and decide whether to get a professional to manage the project for you. Finally, you'd need to work out how to fund the project, and if borrowing is necessary, obtain a **mortgage**.

Ensuring you have enough money to survive and thrive throughout your life is just like building a house. You need to take a step back, think about the big picture and then break it down into a series of manageable and smaller actions.

The key difference between building a house and managing your money is that planning your money is an ongoing, but often less tangible, process.

We call this process **financial planning**, which involves being:

- intentional, structured and disciplined, about defining, measuring and reviewing your current and potential financial situation, and
- thinking about, engaging with and understanding the implications of different actions, to provide the context for day-to-day financial decisions, behaviours and habits.

Having a long-term financial plan improves well-being

A recent study found that people who had a long-term financial plan experienced greater financial well-being. Thinking about their life over many years, rather than just the here and now gave them context for financial decisions and made them feel more in control of day-to-day spending, resulting in lower debt and higher savings (Morningstar, 2017).

> The further ahead a person thinks in time and the clearer their picture of the future, the better their behavior in terms of cash, credit, and savings management. This relationship remains significant when controlling for income, age, and all other demographic factors.
>
> ... we found that a person's perspective on time was far more influential than income, age, education, or gender when it came to personal finances. Our results showed that people who think further into the future tend to save more frequently and build larger savings balances in retirement and non-retirement accounts.
>
> Compared with those with time horizons of less than a year, people with full financial life plans had, on average, 20 times more money

saved. Even looking ahead by just a few years increased savings four-fold.

Our analyses showed time horizon had a significantly greater impact on economic behaviours than income. Yes, a person must have income that is adequate to their needs if they are going to be able to save. Our study suggests, however, that, regardless of paycheck size, having a future-oriented mindset can make the difference between allowing expenses to crowd out one's income or finding ways to save money.

The key point is that you make day-to-day decisions about spending and working in the context of the impact this is likely to have on your long-term financial plan.

As you progress through life you might decide that you need to save more, take more **investment risks** with your capital, work longer or release capital from your home by downsizing. You might even decide to change course completely and head for a different destination.

As Figure 2.5 shows, life doesn't go in a straight line, and stuff happens. A financial plan is merely your best guess of where you want to go in life and how money might support that direction. It isn't a straitjacket!

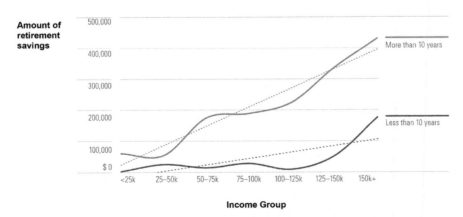

Figure 2.4 Retirement savings by income and mental time horizon

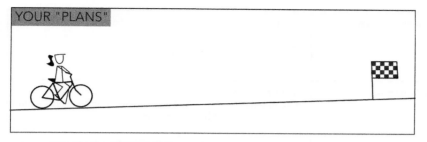

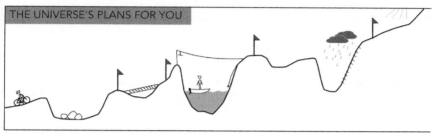

DOGHOUSEDIARIES

Figure 2.5 Life doesn't go in a nice, straight, predictable line
Source: http://thedoghousediaries.com/

Getting started with planning your money

Planning your finances can seem daunting and overwhelming. If you aren't comfortable with numbers and feel bamboozled by financial jargon, it's easy to switch off, particularly given there are any number of other, more enjoyable, activities on which you can spend your time and money.

To help you develop a better money mindset, have a look at the suggestions in Figure 2.6. These have been developed by psychologists based on what research suggests can help people better engage with their finances.

Financial planning priorities

Figure 2.7 sets out, in order of priority, the key financial planning issues you need to consider and take action on.

Take the first step	Visualise your goal. Have a clear sense of where you want to be. Break down how you are going to get there into small steps. Then take one small step towards your goal today.
Make it known	Own up to a fear or problem and share it with someone you trust. Enlist the help of a supportive buddy. Once you've put it out into the world there's more chance of a solution.
Get outside yourself	If you're trapped by **inertia** and indecision, ask yourself 'What would X do?' Think of someone who you believe has it right financially - then put it into action.
The law of opposites	You can trick your brain by behaving in the opposite way to how you feel. So acting as if you are the person you want to be will conquer some of the barriers you've been putting up.
Reframe	Putting a different spin on problems can lead to a fresh approach. If the idea of a pension bores you, for example, reframing it as a gift to your future self could shift your mindset.

Figure 2.6 Psychologists' tips for creating a more positive financial planning mindset

Source: AXA Group 2009.

Activity: Have a look at each item in Figure 2.7 and make a note next to it if you need to look at this area further.

Where do you want to go?

The clearer you are about your values, priorities and any specific goals you wish to achieve, the clearer you'll be about the role of money in your life.

Conventional thinking is that you need to define, quantify and prioritise your financial planning goals. More precisely, they need to be **SMART goals**: specific, measurable, attainable, realistic and time-related. Then each goal can be prioritised based on how important it is to you and whether it is a short, medium or long-term goal.

	Issue	Description	My actions
1	Strategy for repaying any expensive (non-mortgage) debt	Bad debt, in the form of credit cards, overdrafts, catalogue clubs and bank loans are expensive and stop you from building wealth. You need to have a sensible and sustainable plan to repay this type of debt as quickly as possible.	
2	Save for retirement through **workplace pension** scheme	Saving enough to support your lifestyle when you have no (or much less) income from working is essential. See Chapter 6 for further ideas on funding rates.	
3	Protect your family against financial impact of your death	There's a low risk of dying under age 65 but the financial impact on your dependants could be massive. **Life insurance** is usually provided by employers but if you need more it is relatively cheap and will ensure your dependants are financially secure in the event of your premature demise. You'll also need to ensure you keep up-to-date any **death in service benefit** nomination of beneficiaries with your employer. Having a valid **will** ensures against leaving a mess and the right people receive your intended legacy.	
4	**Emergency fund** for unexpected spending	Whether it's losing your job, your car needing repairs or replacing the washing machine, unexpected expenses can throw you off kilter and lead to incurring expensive unsecured debt. Having enough readily accessible cash is key to financial resilience and feeling in control, but not at the expense of repaying any bad debt (see point 1).	
5	Financial impact of illness or disability	If you lose your income because you are unable to work due to illness or disability, this could have a massive impact on your standard of living and longer-term financial security. **Income protection insurance** can plug any gap not covered by your employer.	
6	Funding housing	Buying your own home generally makes good financial sense over the very long term but it might not make sense when you are young or need maximum flexibility. You should consider assistance schemes like Help to Buy, Shared Ownership, Lifetime ISAs, as well as ascertaining whether your family would give or lend you money for a deposit. If you are buying a house with a mortgage you need to regularly review the interest rate, repayment strategy and term.	
7	Saving for any other key life goals	Work out how you'll fund other important life goals, including the tax implications.	
8	Checking whether the taxman will be the biggest beneficiary of your **estate**	If you need and want to minimise the impact of **inheritance tax** on your estate, you'll need to regularly review the numerous (and perfectly legal) planning techniques available and decide what action to take.	

Figure 2.7 Financial planning basics checklist

Source: Author's checklist

If you are below age 35 then most of your goals will probably be short- to **medium-term** ones and as such that is where most of your financial resources will be directed.

Don't worry if you don't have any SMART financial planning goals. It's perfectly OK not to know where you want to go in life, particularly when you are younger. Just make some rough guesses about the general direction you want to take.

Amur's story

Amur is 25 and earns £40,000 as a website coder in Newcastle. He is currently renting an apartment with his girlfriend who is from the UK. Amur's parents live in India and his brother lives in Spain. Amur's main goals are as follows:

- 18 months
  - To maintain existing **cash reserve** of £25,000
  - To gain additional coding skills at cost of £6,000 to increase annual salary by £10,000
- 2–5 years
  - To get married at cost (to me) of £10,000
  - To buy a house with deposit (in today's terms) of £80,000 and balance with a mortgage of c. £320,000
- 10 years+
  - To continue to repay **student loan**
  - To be on track towards financial independence with aim of providing income of about 40% of final salary from age 70.

Behavioural science tells us that we find shorter term goals like buying a house, getting married or travelling the world much more emotionally evocative than more abstract and distant goals like saving for retirement. This makes sense because when you are in your 20s and 30s, 60 seems so far away that you can't really comprehend its relevance and importance financially.

For very long-term goals like retirement it makes sense to start saving as soon as possible but initially at a very low level, while you focus on your shorter-term goals and build your earned income.

Your base plan will include all the goals, regardless of timeframe, which are most important to you. The time frame is when the goal is intended to be achieved, not when you intend to start working towards it.

In the case study of Amur, his goals seem to meet the SMART test. Amur could add other goals until he reaches the point where current and future financial resources are unlikely to be sufficient to fund them.

> **Activity**: Have a think about your own life goals which need money to achieve and write them down in as much detail as you can, including: target date to achieve, amount and how important they are to you.

Goal	Target date	Importance	Amount	Action

Your income and expenditure

Income

In Chapter 1 we looked at the importance to your financial well-being of your income from working and ensuring that you have more income than you spend. If you can't reduce spending, then you must increase your income. You may have other sources of money available to you, over and above salary, at various stages in your life, which could help you to meet your goals. Figure 2.8 shows a range of financial resources other than basic salary from your job.

Personal financial resources			
Overtime	Bonus	Rental income	**Dividends**
Savings interest	Employer pension contributions	Royalties	Inheritance
Tax credits	Child benefit	Pension credit	Housing benefit
Second job	Childcare funding	Selling unwanted possessions	Renting room in your home

Figure 2.8 Personal financial resources
Source: Author's categorisation

You can also increase your financial resources, whether from income or capital, by making sure you are taking advantage of all available **tax reliefs**, **tax exemptions** and **tax allowances**. Think about what other specific actions you can take to increase income or free up capital. Look at the ideas in the box for inspiration.

Ideas to increase income and/or free up capital

- Letting out a room in your home is tax-free to a certain amount (£7,500 per annum in 2018–19) under the **rent-a-room relief** scheme.
  A relatively new **property allowance** lets you have a tax-free income up to £1,000 a year from using your home – for example, renting it out through a website for a couple of weeks or letting out your drive for parking. (But it can't be combined with rent-a-room relief.)
- Similarly, a relatively new **trading allowance** lets you have up to £1,000 of income tax-free from a very small business, for example, selling crafts online or giving music lessons. But this has to be your only business and you can't deduct any expenses.

- Declutter your home and sell (or give away or recycle) what you no longer need. You'd be amazed what people will buy and the cash can help you reduce debt, increase savings or fund an important purchase. Recent estimates are that the typical home has over £3,000 worth of unused possessions.
- Ensure that you are receiving all **state benefits** to which you are entitled such as tax credits.
- Dividends with your **dividend tax allowance** and **interest** earned within your **personal savings allowance**, a pension or individual savings account are tax-free.
- **Private pension** contributions are currently highly tax efficient and could lower your annual tax liability.
- If you have a skill or expertise you might be able to teach this to others in your spare time.
- Some forms of expenditure are deductible from your taxable income such as professional subscriptions, certain **capital expenditure**, and car mileage that hasn't been reimbursed by your employer.
- The bank of mum and dad or granny and grandad could be helpful and one-off gifts of money could be helpful to fund a house purchase or other key goals. If your parents or grandparents have surplus income and they gift this to you on a regular basis, as well as giving you an additional tax-free inflow, it will be immediately free of inheritance tax in the UK.

Activity: Now take a few moments to note how you might increase your surplus income.

Increasing happiness from increasing surplus income	
Tactic	Specific action

Increasing happiness from increasing surplus income	
Tactic	Specific action

Learning how to control and direct your spending

A budget is telling your money where you want to go instead of wondering where it went.

(John C. Maxwell in Ramsey, 2010)

For many people the idea of an expenditure budget is unappealing because it conjures up feelings of limits, restriction and rules. It also takes some effort to work out exactly where your money currently goes and then decide what you should or could spend your income on.

Working out what you spend your money on and devising a budget you can live with is essential to getting control of your day-to-day finances and helping you avoid bad debt and build financial capital.

US financial wellness firm HelloWallet (HelloWallet, 2014) found that, when comparing workers on the same wages, those who tracked their finances using the HelloWallet digital personal finance system had about $150,000 higher net wealth than workers who did not monitor their spending budget.

In order to avoid incurring 'bad' debt (spending on things that are not assets) you must ensure that your net of tax income is in balance with your combined expenditure.

The key financial planning principle that I learnt was 'spend less than you earn'. A much more empowering way of achieving the same thing is telling yourself to 'earn more than you spend'. Either way, money in must balance with money going out if you are to become financially stable and have choices in life.

How to budget

First work out what you currently spend money on each month by looking at your bank statement or, if you use one, a money app. Make sure to account for all those 'one off' items that have a habit of recurring. Figure 2.9 sets out a range of spending items to help you remember.

To help you take control of your spending you might find it helpful to think about your personal expenses falling into one of three categories:

- **BASIC YOU**: This is your core living costs including: housing, transport, food, regular bills, insurance premiums and any other 'essential' ongoing expenses.

Sources of expenditure			
Alcohol	Takeaway food	Taxis	Takeaway coffee
Cinema & entertainment	Transport (including season ticket)	Cosmetics & beauty	Eating out
Smoking	Digital apps & gaming	Broadband & mobile phone	Insurance premiums
Pension contributions	Non-pension savings	Debt repayments	Clothes
Food	Utility bills	Household goods	Repairs & maintenance

Figure 2.9 Sources of expenditure

Source: Author's categorisation

- **FUTURE YOU**: This is the money you are using to: reduce debts, save for an emergency fund, and invest for the long term (including through your workplace pension).
- **FUN YOU**: This is the money you spend on all the luxuries and extras that make life more comfortable, interesting, exciting or varied including: socialising, eating out, non-essential clothes, holidays, trips, takeaway drinks and food, books, hobbies and any other possessions or experiences from which you derive pleasure and enjoyment.

Some financial planners suggest fixed percentages for each of the spending categories, such as 50% for BASIC YOU, 20% for FUTURE YOU and 30% for FUN YOU.

The problem with this approach is it takes no account of the cost of living where you live. For example, London housing is much more expensive than northern Scotland. Nor does it reflect your own priorities and life stage. For example, you might have just started work, be renting a cheap room in a house and want (and need) to do a lot of socialising to make new friends and have fun.

I suggest that you tot up all your BASIC YOU expenditure and then split whatever income is left 40% to FUTURE YOU and 60% to FUN YOU.

The UK's free financial **guidance** service has a useful online expenses calculator to help you identify potential savings, if you find that the amount available for FUTURE YOU and FUN YOU is too small. You can find it here: www.moneyadviceservice.org.uk/en/tools/quick-cash-finder/calculators.

You then need to have two bank current accounts:

- Account 1 has a **debit card** that you KEEP IN A DRAWER AT HOME, and it has a small overdraft facility.
- Account 2 has a debit card but NO OVERDRAFT FACILITY.
- Your salary is paid into Account 1 and on the same day that account transfers an amount equal to the FUN YOU budget into account 2.

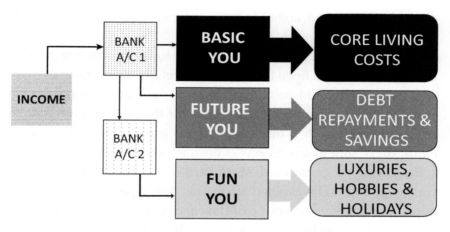

Figure 2.10 The Smart Spending System™
Source: Author's diagram

- On the next day Account 1 pays all the debt repayment and regular saving as per the FUTURE YOU budget amount.
- The balance of what's left in Account 1 is there to meet all the BASIC YOU monthly expenses.
- All the FUN YOU expenditure throughout the month must be paid from Account 2, either via debit card, cash or cheque.

This budgeting approach – which I call the Smart Spending System – is shown visually in Figure 2.10. Once you get this system set up IT WILL TRANSFORM YOUR LIFE and you will to need to expend minimal effort in controlling your spending.

Other planning points

Good debt not bad debt

Debt can be used responsibly to enable you to invest in yourself (like education or skills) or acquire assets like property (as long as it brings in more than it costs). Whatever the reasons for which you borrow money, remember two things: interest is a definite and regular cost that will reduce your ability to save and the capital must eventually be repaid.

Although current global interest rates are low, they may not stay like that forever and you need to think very carefully about the impact on your expenditure if interest rates were, say, three times higher than at present (as they have been in the past). For this reason, even though buying a home with a mortgage can be a good long-term use of funds, make sure that you don't overstretch yourself.

Borrowing on credit card, **store card** or **payday loans** to finance consumption is to be avoided at all costs. This type of borrowing will be a continual drain on your **cashflow** and will hold back your ability to accumulate assets that generate cashflow. Borrowing is discussed in more detail in Chapter 7 and getting help with debt is discussed in Chapter 8.

Action: Once you have got a budget and brought spending below what you earn, review any existing bad debt to refinance it with lower cost borrowing and a repayment schedule that will eradicate the debt in the shortest time frame possible. But make sure the monthly payments are affordable and sustainable, otherwise you'll just slip further into debt.

Bank of mum and dad

An interest-free loan from your family is the cheapest form of borrowing and payday loans are the most expensive. As a general rule you should avoid debt, but otherwise repay it as fast as possible, starting with the most expensive debt.

Action: Raise the issue of personal finance with your parents and grandparents and explain what you would do with any inheritance that they might be willing and able to give you now, rather than when they die. If they know you'd use the money wisely your relatives might be more inclined to provide financial help sooner rather than later.

Invest in yourself

In addition to cultivating a positive mental 'can do' attitude, increasing your relevant skills, knowledge and experience is the best way to increase your earning power. It therefore makes sense to look for ways to invest in your capability, whether attending business school, evening classes, distance learning or day release by your employer.

Action: Investigate the training and development opportunities available to you, either through your employer or independently.

Don't rush to buy property

Although buying your own home generally makes more sense than renting over the long term, avoid rushing to buy a house until you have established your earning power, know where you want to live (which may be dictated by your work) and have a clearer idea of who, if anyone, will be your life partner.

Buying and selling property can be expensive, and if you have to sell at a time when the value of the property has fallen and your equity is reduced, it can set you back years.

Action: Think carefully about where you want to live and work and whether buying a home makes sense from a practical and financial perspective.

Keep it simple stupid (KISS)

Keep your personal financial planning as simple as possible.

If it looks too good

If anyone tells you that an investment is virtually risk-free and will generate a 20%-a-year return, give them a wide berth. *If it looks too good to be true, then it probably is.*

Tax isn't everything

You need to avoid becoming obsessed about avoiding tax. By all means minimise your tax bill by using all the legitimate and tried and tested products and solutions available, but not to such an extent that you don't have enough money to live on today or fall foul of the tax authorities and end up paying penalties and fines.

The media is not your friend

The media, in the form of newspapers, 24-hour news, websites or magazines, is not designed to help you to make good decisions. It focuses on what personal finance professionals call 'noise' or 'financial pornography' in the form of negative stories or sensationalist 'get rich quick' ideas because they are newsworthy.

People who participate in such media comment are chosen because they make the media outlet more marketable, not because of their insight. In general, the news is not the truth but a form of entertainment, so remember that when forming your opinions about money.

> **Action**: Tune out the 'noise' of the media in relation to your finances. Think in terms of many decades, not days.

Conclusion

We've discussed the importance of making working and spending decisions in the context of what's important to you and what will maximise your financial well-being.

Developing an overall financial plan, maximising your human capital and learning to control spending are essential foundations to being good with money and living a flourishing life.

In the following chapters, we'll look at some of the various elements of planning your finances in a little more detail, so you have the confidence and capability to make better decisions throughout your working life and beyond.

Note

1   © 2017 Morningstar, Inc. All Rights Reserved. The information contained herein: (1) is proprietary to Morningstar and/or its content providers; (2) may not be copied or distributed; (3) does not constitute investment advice offered by Morningstar; and (4) is not warranted to be accurate, complete or timely. Neither Morningstar nor its content providers are responsible for any damages or losses arising from any use of this information. Past performance is no guarantee of future results. Use of information from Morningstar does not necessarily constitute agreement by Morningstar, Inc. of any investment philosophy or strategy presented in this publication.

References

AXA Group (2009) *The Psychological Forces and Barriers that Influence People's Financial Management* [online] www.sheconomics.com/downloads/AXA_Report.pdf (accessed 27 February 2018).

Gratton, L. and Scott, A. (2017) *The 100-Year Life: Living and Working in an Age of Longevity*, p.2. Bloomsbury.

HelloWallet (2014) 'Infographic: the power of budgeting'. [online] http://info.hellowallet.com/201403HBConference_LPBudgetingInfographic Orange.html (accessed 1 March 2018).

Morningstar (2017) *When More is Less: Rethinking Financial Health* [online] http://images.mscomm.morningstar.com/Web/MorningstarInc/%7b-b87a29d4-9264-4e6f-a5d7-5e65f8714f92%7d_US_ADV_MoreLess_Whitepaper_Final.pdf (accessed 29 February 2018).

Ramsey, D. (2010) *The Money Answer Book*. Thomas Nelson.

Building resilience and wealth through saving

Lien Luu

In a nutshell:

- **Building up a buffer of savings is the best way to guard against falling into debt.**
- **The secret to long-term security and achievement of goals lies in saving and investing.**
- **Successful wealth creation requires paying yourself first and automating the saving process.**
- **You may be able to take advantage of saving schemes at work.**

> Wealth lies not in having great possessions, but in having few wants.
> —Epictetus

As you saw in Chapter 2, some goals are critical to your well-being, such as paying off debts, having an emergency fund, protecting your family from the effects of death and ill health, and saving for retirement. These should take priority in your financial planning.

Once these fundamentals are in place, you might like to pursue other goals that are more aspirational and 'nice-to-have' and thus have a lower priority, such as taking time off work to travel the world, leaving an inheritance, or even buying a yacht.

Whether essential or aspirational, some goals may require a large lump sum of money, equivalent to months, or in many cases, years, of salary. To get your hands on this sum of money, you can either borrow or use your savings. Borrowing is acceptable in certain circumstances, such as for house purchase, home improvements or buying a car. However, borrowing can rapidly spiral into problem debt if it is taken out to pay for everyday essentials or items that do not increase in value (such as, the weekly shop, Christmas presents or endless clothes and gadgets). Building up savings is therefore a more robust and sustainable way of allowing you to pay for things without resorting to debt.

Saving implies that our income is surplus to our requirements. In reality, many of us (irrespective of level of income) do not have surplus income unless we exercise discipline explicitly in order to save.

Topics such as managing debt, protecting your income and your family, and saving for retirement are covered in later chapters. This chapter examines how to save and invest for other goals, starting with the critical goal of building an emergency fund.

Having an emergency fund

All days are not same. Save for a rainy day. When you don't work, savings will work for you.

—M.K. Soni

One of the essential saving goals is to build an emergency fund, so that you can pay for unexpected bills such as a boiler breakdown, car repair, dental treatment, or a short spell of unemployment, without having to resort to expensive debt. Unexpected costs, such as car repairs or a new boiler, can be expensive, ranging from £1,000 to £2,500 (Kirkland, 2017).

Many households in the UK simply do not have adequate savings to deal with the unexpected. In fact, the BBC reported in September 2016 that more than 16 million people in the UK had savings of less than £100 (Milligan, 2016). Worryingly, the number of households without any savings is growing. In 2017, Money Charity found that around 9.45 million (35%) households had no savings in the UK.

Table 3.1 Example cost of some unexpected bills

Types of repairs	Cost
Car maintenance costs	£1,130–£2,440
New boiler	£1,000–£2,500

By June 2018, this number had increased to nearly 10 million households, equivalent to a total of 15.5 million adults, and nearly 36% of UK households (Money Charity, 2018a and Hughes, 2018).

Indeed, a study by the Royal Society of Arts shows that economic insecurity has become the 'new normal' in the UK. In a survey of more than 2,000 workers, it was found that 70% were 'chronically broke', with 40% confessing that their finances were permanently precarious and 30% not managing to get by. According to the report, those who had some savings only had a modest level: 32% surveyed had less than £500 and 41% less than £1,000 (*The Guardian*, January 2018). Many households in the UK are in a vulnerable position and would not be able to pay for the cost of repairs, such as a car or boiler breakdown, let alone withstand the impact of major financial shocks.

> **Action**: Work out how much your household spends per month. Then calculate how many months of expenditure you want to have in your emergency fund to make you feel secure.

As a general rule of thumb, it is recommended that you should have an emergency fund equal to between 3 or 12 months' expenditure/income (whichever is higher). For example, suppose your estimated monthly expenditure is £2,600, then an emergency fund of £7,800–£24,000 is recommended.

Your emergency fund should be held in fairly liquid assets (such as cash deposits or National Savings accounts), so that you can access the money when you need it. Having this fund will give you peace of mind, knowing that you can pay for emergencies and unexpected bills.

Other goals

After paying off expensive debts, setting up an emergency fund, funding a workplace pension and protecting your family in the event of your death or long-term illness, you may want to save for other goals.
Goals can be classified into:

- Short-term goals (less than 5 years): include annual overseas holiday, new car, home improvements and money for Christmas.
- Medium-term goals (5–10 years): include paying for wedding, a house deposit, holiday home, or school and university fees.
- According to the Association of Investment Companies (AIC), if parents had saved just £50 a month in the average investment company for the past 18 years they would have £32,500 by July 2017. Those able to invest £100 a month would now be sitting on over £65,000 (Lunn, 2018).

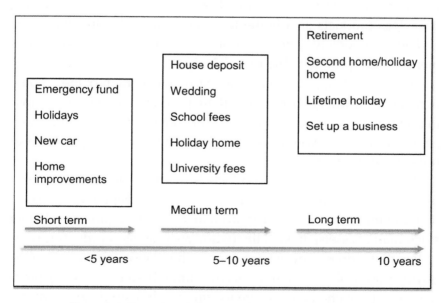

Figure 3.1 Examples of short-, medium- and long-term goals

Source: Author's chart

- Long-term goals (10+ years): include saving for retirement, buying a second home, paying for a holiday of a lifetime, setting up a business or taking early retirement.

In addition, many of us aspire to achieve **financial freedom** – a life when you have sufficient resources to meet your needs and have the means to do what you like. You also only work because you love to.

Financial freedom is very powerful because it confers many intangible benefits such as peace of mind, financial security, and the freedom and flexibility to live and work on your own terms. Without money worries, you also have less stress, sleep better and can focus on other enjoyable aspects of life.

Just imagine your life when you do not have to worry about money!

Saving versus investing

In general, if your goals are **short term**, then you should be looking at savings products as a home for your money. This includes bank and building society savings accounts and National Savings & Investments (NS&I) products. The reason is that the amount of money you pay in does not fall, so you can be reasonably certain of the amount of money you will get back. Thus, these products are ideal for savings that you may need back either at short notice (such as your emergency fund) or that you'll need to cash in fairly soon (to pay for your holiday, new car, and so on).

The downside of savings products is that the interest they earn is usually low and, as you'll see a bit later in this chapter, much lower than the return you can expect from investments (**equities** and other stock-market assets). In fact, the return from savings products is often so low that it doesn't even keep pace with inflation, meaning that the buying power of your money falls over time. Therefore, savings products are a poor choice if you are looking at a long-term goal; instead, the wise choice is investments.

Informal saving schemes: money pools

In some countries, you can borrow from people you know, through a system of **money pools**. A group of people contribute on a regular basis to a common fund and members take turns collecting the resulting lump sum. So, for example, ten people might contribute £100 each month to a money pool and take turns collecting £1,000 each over ten months.

Money pools are one of the world's oldest savings mechanisms, started over 1,000 years ago. They have many names – Fokontany in Madagascar, Hui in Taiwan, Pandero in Peru, and Cundina in Mexico (Poptech, 2014, and PayPal).

Money pools are found in the UK, often in ethnic groups who have carried on the tradition from their original countries of origin. PayPal has recently launched *Moneypools* to allow people to borrow money through this method.

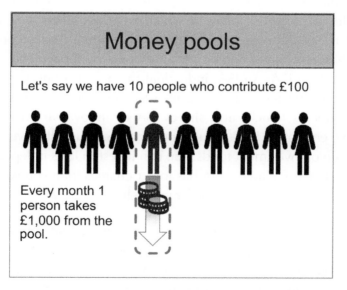

Figure 3.2 Example of how a money pool works

Source: Adapted from Elaine Baruwa (2015)

How your employer may help you save

You will usually be saving for retirement through your workplace (see Chapter 6). But you may also have access to other types of saving scheme, in particular:

- Workplace credit union: A credit union is a mutual organisation run by its members for its members that offers both savings products and loans (and sometimes other products too like a current account). All the members of a credit union must have a common bond. Sometimes this is living in the same area or going to the same place of worship, but often the bond is that all the members work for the same employer. A savings account with a credit union can start with as little as £1 and the interest you receive, although typically low, might be higher than what you get from a high street bank. A credit union can also be a source of relatively cheap loans and can lend money to members who do not necessarily meet the criteria for borrowing from high street lenders such as banks and building societies, many of which have tightened their lending criteria as a consequence of the credit crunch. Loans come with no hidden charges and no penalties for early repayment.
- Workplace ISA: An ISA (individual savings account) is a tax-free scheme that lets you invest in a savings account (cash ISA) or investments (**stocks** and **shares** ISA or innovative finance ISA). Some employers have set up workplace ISAs, usually investing in a choice of investment funds. You can invest in ISAs independently, but often a workplace ISA has lower charges than you would pay for an ISA that you arrange for yourself.

A big plus with workplace savings schemes is that your employer usually has an arrangement that means your regular saving is taken direct from your salary and paid into your workplace credit union savings account or ISA before you get the rest of your pay. Automating your saving in this way helps you stick to your saving plans.

You can read more about these and other types of workplace savings schemes at Money Advice Service.*

Household finances in the UK

Money is tight for many households. In the UK, around 67% are employed, relying on a salary as their main source of income. Many UK households (42%) rely on just one income (Hughes, 2018). The average income in the UK in 2017 was £27,300 per annum. HMRC tax statistics show that in 2017–18 more than 62% had income of £20,000 or under, and another 34.6% between £20,000 and £50,000. The overwhelming majority (97%) then had an income of £50,000 a year or less, and only a tiny minority 0.05% earned in excess of £1 million.

There is a gap between income and spending level in the UK. While the average income was £27,300 per year in 2017, the average level of expenditure is estimated at £28,813 and £31,272 per year, giving an annual shortfall of between £1,500 and nearly £4,000 (ONS, 2017b; Aviva, 2017a). To bridge the difference between income and spending, many households borrow and the average consumer credit

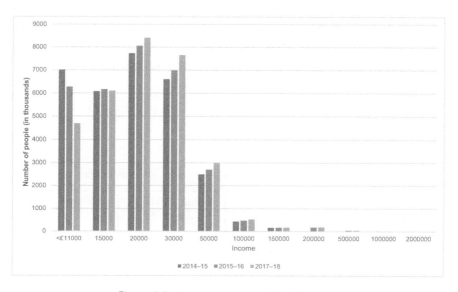

Figure 3.3a Income range in UK, 2014–18

Source: HMRC, UK Income Tax Liabilities Statistics (2017, 2018)

debt in the UK is around £8,000 per person (not including mortgage) (Brignall, 2017; Money Charity, June 2018).

For those households who manage to save, the level is quite modest. Research by Aviva shows that households save on average £103 per month (£1,236 annually), assuming average monthly net income is £2,709 and expenditure £2,606. However, they could save more by reducing their monthly expenditure, say to £2,451, giving them a monthly saving of £155. If they live on the absolute minimum of £1,904 per month, then there is the potential to save £702 per month (Aviva, 2017a).

There is a significant difference in the level of savings between low- and high-income families. Research by Aviva shows that a typical low-income family (classified as those earning £1,500 or less a month) had less than £100 of savings in 2016–17, while a high-income family had more than £62,000. Low-income families, thus, are much more exposed to financial shocks (Aviva, 2017b).

Many households in the UK, thus, cannot afford to pay for many of their goals out of surplus income. They therefore need to save to pay for their goals, such as Christmas presents and a family holiday. The cost of a wedding or a new car would take years of saving. If households can only save £103 per month, it would also take households more than six years to save £7,500 (the amount required to cover three months of average expenditure).

Table 3.2a Savings level of low- and high-income families

	Winter 2015/16	Winter 2016/17	Difference (%)
Low-income families	£136	£95	-30%
High- income families	£50,208	£62,885	25%
Difference	£50,072	£62,790	25%

Source: Aviva (2017b)

Table 3.2b Costs of major expenses

Goals	Typical costs	Comments
Christmas	£753	Includes presents (£358), food & drink (£183), parties (£109), and Christmas tree and decorations (£83)
Annual holiday	£6,608	£4,792 for family of four + £227 per person spending money per week away
Weddings	£27,161	Some regions cost more
New car	£33,359	Lifetime cost of a car estimated at £207,000

Sources: Evolutionmoney (2018); Go Compare (2016); Shale-Hester (2018); Hull (2018); Young (2017).

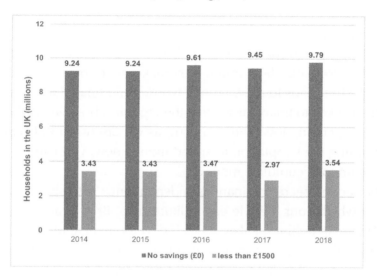

Figure 3.3b Number of households with no or low savings
Source: Money Charity, June 2018

What steps do you need to take to save money?

In order to achieve goals, it is essential to save. Indeed, research shows that the ability to save and invest is the engine of wealth accumulation and the attainment of financial independence. In his classic *The Richest Man in Babylon*, George Clason explains that saving (10% of income) and controlling expenditures are the first two fundamental steps of wealth accumulation.

The authors of *The Millionaire Next Door* (Stanley and Danko, 2010), after studying more than 1,000 millionaires in the US between 1995 and 1996, also reach the same conclusions – the secrets of financial freedom lie in planning, controlling consumption (budgeting), and being frugal and actively investing (15% of income). If households in the UK typically save only 5% of their income (Money Charity, 2017), they therefore need to double or treble their level of saving.

Many people, however, find it is difficult to save, due to Parkinson's Law (named after C. Northcote Parkinson). This law states that, no matter how much money people earn, some people tend to spend the entire amount. Their expenses rise as their earnings increase.

Despite earning much more than they were earning in their first jobs, they seem to spend every single penny to maintain their current lifestyle. No matter how much they make, there never seems to be enough. This leads to debt, money worries and financial frustration.

The first key to financial success then requires breaking Parkinson's Law, by spending less than you earn, as we discussed in Chapter 2. By resisting the temptation to spend money now, you can then save and begin to accumulate money.

The second secret of financial independence is to slow down the rate at which your lifestyle expenditure rises. Brian Tracy, a Canadian-American public speaker and self-development author, calls it the 'wedge'. If you can drive a wedge between your earnings and the costs of your lifestyle, and then save and invest the difference, you can continue to improve your lifestyle as you make more money.

He concludes that: 'If you allow your expenses to increase at a slower rate than your earnings, and you save or invest the difference, you will become financially independent in your working lifetime' (Tracy, 2018).

Brian Tracy therefore recommends two actions:

- First, stop all non-essential expenses, and draw up a budget of your fixed, unavoidable costs per month and aim to limit your expenditures temporarily to these amounts. Then you carefully examine every expense and look for ways to economize or cut back. Aim for a minimum of a 10% reduction in your living costs over the next three months.

- Second, learn to save and invest 50% of any increase in your earnings from any source, and commit to live on the rest. This still leaves you the other 50% to spend how you want, and do this for the rest of your career (Tracy, 2018).

How do you successfully save?

When you earn money, it is easier to spend rather than save. Saving requires discipline, planning and determination, and as Brigham Young said (quoted in Crampton, 2017):

> If you wish to get rich, save what you get. A fool can earn money; but it takes a wise man to save and dispose of it to his own advantage.

So, how do you save? Successful saving requires you to take seven steps.

Have a savings goal

To be successful at saving, you first need to decide what you want to save for. Money, after all, is only a means to an end. What are your motivations to save – a new car or a once in a lifetime holiday at an exotic destination? A new house?

Whatever your goals are, as we touched on in Chapter 2, ideally these need to be SMART goals.

- **S**pecific: Smart goals are specific enough to suggest action: 'Save money to take my family to Disneyland Florida, pay for flight and accommodation and spending money'.
- **M**easurable: Create goals that can be measured. 'I need to save £3,000 to pay for flight costs and £2,000 for spending money'.
- **A**ttainable: Goals need to be reasonable. 'I need to save £350 per month for 24 months'.

- **R**ealistic: The goals need to make sense. 'I can save £350 per month by reducing my spending or getting a part-time job or working more hours'.
- **T**ime-related: Set a definite target date. 'I can save £8,000 over a 24-month period'.

Visualise your goals

Once you set the goals, you need to visualise them to increase your motivation and determination to achieve. Successful people use visualisation techniques to focus on their goals and desires and ensure the achievement of desired outcomes, because, as Jack Canfield highlighted, visualisation technique accomplishes four very important things (Canfield, 2017):

1. It activates your creative subconscious – you begin to generate creative ideas to achieve your goal.
2. It programmes your brain – so that it is able to recognise the resources you will need to achieve your dreams.
3. It activates the law of attraction – thus drawing into your life the people, resources, and circumstances you will need to achieve your goals.
4. It builds your internal motivation – to take the necessary actions to achieve your dreams.

Start early

Whatever your saving goals are, you need to start early and take advantage of **compound interest**. This is especially important for long-term saving such as retirement.

Let's demonstrate this using an example. Samantha starts saving at the age of 21, investing £1,000 per year with 8% growth and stops at the age of 30. Her twin sister, Lizy, starts at the age of 30, paying £1,000 per year with 8% growth and continues until age 65. At the age of 65, Samantha has built a pot of savings of £225,951, while Lizy, despite paying in more, has a smaller pot of £187,102. Thus, the

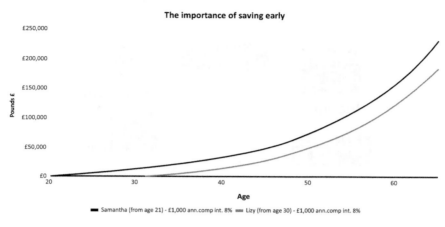

Figure 3.4 Importance of saving early
Source: Author's illustration

length of time of investment is critical to the size of the final accumulated fund.

Pay yourself first

The trick to ensure that you do save every month is using a technique called *pay yourself first*. This involves putting aside a percentage (10–15%) of your income before you start spending. You need to transfer the money into a separate bank account.

As Warren Buffet, one of the richest men in the world, advises (quoted in Millennial Finance Blog, 2018):

> Do not save what is left after spending, but spend what is left after saving.

Automate the process

After deciding on the percentage to save, you need to automate it. To overcome procrastination and behavioural aspects, the author of

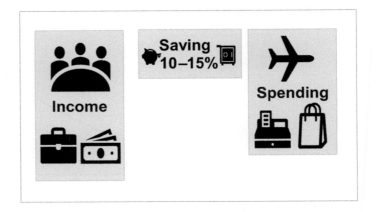

Figure 3.5 Recommended percentage of income to pay yourself first
Source: Author's illustration

Automatic Millionaire, David Bach, suggests that the process must be *automated*. On an individual level, you can automate saving by setting up a **direct debit** or standing order system.

To automate saving for retirement, auto-enrolment was introduced in the UK in 2012. Savings for retirement are automatically deducted from monthly salary, unless employees opt out.

Some employers set up one or more types of workplace savings schemes that enable regular savings to be made through payroll deductions. This means the money goes into the savings account before you receive it, thus reducing the chance of you spending it.

Budget

One way to increase the amount available for saving is to reduce your expenses. This requires drawing up a budget and regularly going through each item of expenditure and seeing how you can cut down. Chapter 2 explained the process of budgeting and I just want to stress here some of the traps we all fall into when it comes to spending.

You need to be aware of expenditure on small items. In the *Automatic Millionaire*, David Bach illustrates how the 'latte factor' can prevent us from achieving our financial goals. Although the daily amount spent on items such as coffee, bottled water, cigarettes,

soft drinks and snacks might seem small and trivial, the accumulated effect can be enormous. As Benjamin Franklin had warned us:
'Beware of little expenses. A small leak will sink a great ship'.

A breakdown of weekly expenditure in the UK is shown in Table 3.3.
This shows spending on recreation and culture, restaurants and
hotels, clothing and footwear, and alcohol and narcotics makes up
nearly 30% of total weekly expenditure.

However, if we categorize the expenses into essential and non-essential, there might be room for saving and we can live on much
less than £554 per week. Table 3.4 suggests a few ideas to reduce
expenses.

Table 3.3 Types of household expenditure, 2016–17

Year 2016–17	£ per week	% of weekly spending
Essential		
Transport	£79.70	14.4
Housing (net), fuel and power	£72.60	13.1
Food and non-alcoholic drinks	£58.00	10.5
Miscellaneous goods and services	£41.80	7.5
Household goods and services	£39.30	7.1
Communication	£17.20	3.1
Health	£7.30	1.3
Education	£5.70	1.0
Sub-total	**£321.60**	**58**
Non-essential		
Recreation and culture	£73.50	13.3
Other expenditure items	£72.00	13.0
Restaurants and hotels	£50.10	9.0
Alcoholic drinks, tobacco and narcotics	£11.90	2.0
Clothing and footwear	£25.10	4.5
Sub-total	**£232.60**	**42**
Total	**£554.20**	**100**

Source: Office for National Statistics (2017b)

Table 3.4 Some ways to reduce spending

Expenses	How
Put savings as the top priority of your spending plan	Increase your pension contributions.
	Take every opportunity to save. Set aside £5 from your wallet/purse a month and then put in the bank every month.
	When you get a rise, increase your savings.
	Put any tax refund into your saving account.
Fees and charges	Make sure you do not pay unnecessary fee and bank charges.
Food at home	Shop with a list and buy only items on the list. Buy sale items. Don't shop on empty stomach.
	Take time to plan your meals. Research shows that this enables families to live on less.
Food away from home	Food away from home costs a lot more, and therefore cutting down on this saves you money. Start with taking a packed lunch to work. It is healthier and cheaper.
	When you eat out, use coupons or discounts.
Alcoholic beverages and tobacco	These are **discretionary expenses** and should be reduced where possible.
Housing	Find ways to reduce your mortgage costs.
	Overpaying your mortgage might allow you to pay off the mortgage early and save on interest payments.
	If you are renting, a house share can save you money.
	Save energy costs by using energy efficient bulbs. Switch off all lights when not in use and unplug electronics.
Clothing	Studies show that most people wear 20% of their clothes 80% of the time. Resist the urge to buy more clothes.
	Reduce clothing costs by shopping at the end of the season for bargains or shopping at discount stores.
Transport	Explore car pooling to save money.
	Drive safely to keep insurance costs down.
	Maintain your car properly to save money on repairs.
Entertainment	This is discretionary expense. There are many low-cost ways of enjoying yourself including visiting museums for free, hiking. Instead of seeing the latest movie, wait for the DVD, and perhaps borrow from your library.
	Electronics prices go down and so do not buy the latest model to save money.

Table 3.4 Continued

Expenses	How
Gifts	Buy them out-of-season such as after Christmas, at the end of the summer or end of winter.
Taxes	Pay your taxes on time to avoid penalties.
	Ensure you claim tax allowances and that you pay the right amount of tax.

Source: Bellevue Community College, *Personal Money Management*, 2008

Use cash

It is also believed that we spend less if we use cash instead of a credit card. One famous experiment found that people were willing to pay almost 80% more for a baseball ticket when using credit instead of cash. This is because you just swipe and do not have to think about it (Money Magazine, 2018).

When using a credit card, we tend to spend more because we do not feel the pain of paying. The easy availability of credit is typically blamed for the spending problem and thus one way to control spending is to use cash, which causes more pain when we spend it (Cheema and Soman, 2008; Rick et al., 2008).

Invest

In the long term, it is difficult to achieve your goals without some kinds of investments. These are important because they provide an additional stream of income, known as **passive income**, which is not dependent on your ability to earn.

If you have to work for your money, there is a limit on the number of jobs you can have. However, if the income is not dependent on your labour and time, you can have an unlimited number of different sources of income. This explains why rich people tend to have multiple sources of income.

Investments can take the form of letting a property, buying shares or **gilts**, and setting up a business. They are different from savings in that you commit to a longer timescale and take more risks, in return for higher rewards.

Saving is seen as a lower risk because your money or capital is relatively safe, and you do not need to worry about losing money overnight.

Investing, on the other hand, gives a higher prospect of a better return, but your capital might not be safe as the value can fluctuate.

People then often save for short-term goals to ensure that the capital value does not go down but invest for long-term goals as this provides opportunities for capital growth and protection against inflation.

The main types of investment

When you invest your money, there are four main types of asset: cash, **bond**/fixed income, property and equity. These vary in levels of risk and reward and meet different investment needs.

Cash is often perceived as the safest asset with a lower risk of **capital loss**. Thus, people tend to hold emergency fund or money for short-term goals in a deposit account.

However, returns, in the form of interest, are low and the value of cash can be eroded by inflation. If interest on your cash is 1% but inflation is 2%, the value of your capital is eroded by 1% every year.

Fixed income and bonds offer better returns than cash. This takes the form of lending money to the government (known as gilts) or to companies (bonds). In addition to income from interest, gilts or bonds also provide opportunities for capital growth and some protection against inflation.

The third asset type is property. Property can provide returns in the form of income and capital growth and protection against inflation. However, one drawback is that it is an **illiquid** asset and it might not be easy to sell when you need the money, unless you invest in a property fund.

The fourth type of asset is equities – part shares in companies. These are often preferred because they usually provide returns in the form of income and capital growth, and protection against long-term inflation. They are also relatively liquid and can be sold to convert their value into cash when needed.

In order to accumulate wealth, it is imperative that you invest surplus income, rather than just save it. This is because, as Table 3.5 shows, equities tend to outperform gilts and cash as well as preserve the purchasing power of money over the very long term.

Table 3.6 emphasises another important message: the significance of re-investment. When you invest in companies by buying shares, you receive dividends. If you re-invest the dividends rather than spend them, the reinvestment magnifies the total return.

However, equities come with risks and so to balance the needs of capital growth with preservation of capital, many investors see fixed interest and equities as the key building blocks of their portfolio.

Table 3.5 Investment returns from different assets

Real investment returns (% p.a.)				
Year	Equities	Gilts	Index-linked	Cash
1977–1987	12.00	4.5		3.4
1987–1997	10.4	6.9		4.6
1997–2007	3.1	3.3	3.7	2.5
2007–2017	3.2	4.0	4.0	-1.9

Source: Barclays, *Equity Gilt Study* 2018, p.93

Table 3.6 Nominal and real returns of assets

Today's value of £100 invested at the end of 1945 without reinvesting income			Today's value of £100 invested at the end of 1945, gross income reinvested		
	Nominal	**Real**		**Nominal**	**Real**
Equities	£10,933	£288	**Equities**	£238,690	£6,294
Gilts	£69	£1.81	**Gilts**	£8,900	£234
			Cash	£6,317	£166

Source: Barclays, *Equity Gilt Study* 2018, p.96

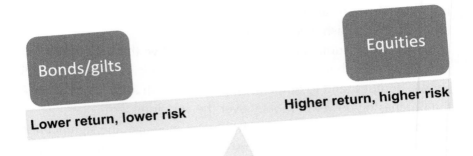

Figure 3.6 The risk–return trade-off
Source: Authors' chart

When they are young, investors can take more risks and so can afford to invest a higher proportion in equities. As they get older, they tend to allocate a higher proportion to bonds/gilts and a lower proportion to equities.

Ownership of assets in the UK

Only a small proportion of households in the UK own shares directly, although most of us own shares indirectly through life insurance, pensions and investment funds. The proportion of shares held directly by individuals in the UK declined between 1963 and 2016. In 1963, individuals owned 54% of UK quotes shares in terms of total value (ONS, 2014). By 2016, this had declined to 12.3%.

Why people make bad saving and investment decisions

In the UK, research shows that many DIY investors prefer **active funds** – funds chosen by an investment manager with the goal of outperforming a benchmark index.

Table 3.7 Shareholdings by individuals in the UK, 2010–16

At 31 December								
	Percent				£ (in billions)			
	2010	2012	2014	2016	2010	2012	2014	2016
Rest of the world	43.1	53.3	53.7	53.9	789.5	933.2	1,073.6	1,100.5
Individuals	10.6	10.6	12.4	12.3	194.6	184.6	247.5	251.5

Source: ONS (2016)

Data obtained by Tilney Bestinvest shows the number of DIY investors on their platform rose from 6,185 in 2012 to 28,308 in 2016, but the percentage of total fund sales for **passive funds** fell from 9% to 8.5% (Romeo, 2017). However, evidence shows that investors tend to under-perform the market.

Research by Dalbar shows that in the US, an average investor achieved 7.26% return over one year, compared to 11.96% return from S&P 500 Index, an underperformance of 4.7% in 2016 (Allen and Hebner, 2017)

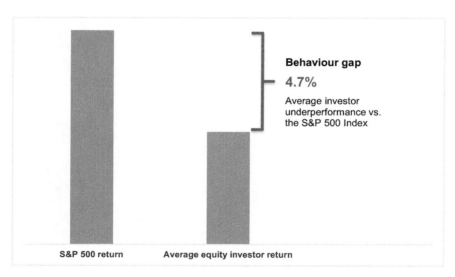

Figure 3.7 The behaviour gap

Source: Allen and Hebner (2017)

The Dalbar study also looks at the performance over the 30-year period between 1987 and 2016. During this period, the average investor achieved 3.99%, while the S&P 500 Index obtained an average return of 10.16%. If the investor had invested $100,000 in 1987, the average investor would have made $322,000 while the same investment in S&P 500 would result in a return of over $2 million, over-performing by nearly seven times (Allen and Hebner).

One of the main reasons why DIY investors under-perform the market is due to their innate behavioural biases, such as **herding**, optimism, **loss aversion**, and **anchoring**. These may contribute to poor investment decisions.

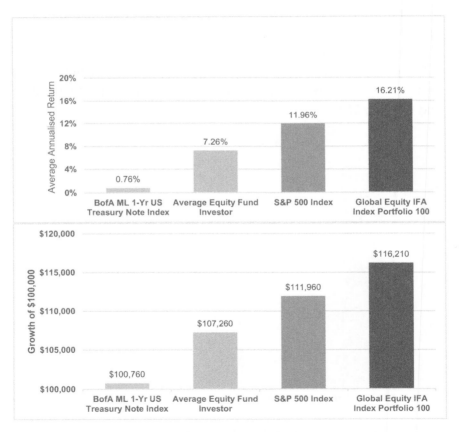

Figure 3.8 One year of average return of investor versus index

Source: Allen and Hebner (2017)

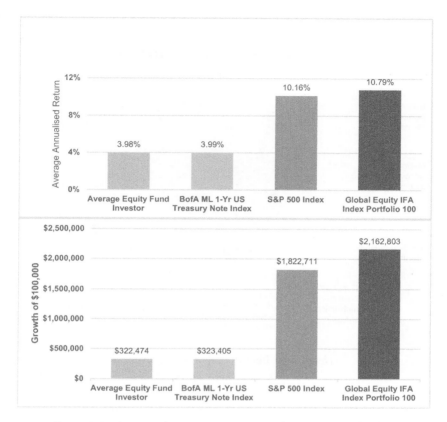

Figure 3.9 30 years of average equity return by investor and index.
While some may question the accuracy of Dalbar's data, this illustration
merely seeks to highlight the difficulty of beating the market

Source: Allen and Hebner (2017)

One major reason for investment under-performance is irrational investor behaviour. When prices rise, we feel optimistic and so we buy more. It is ironic that when it comes to investments, we only feel confident to buy when prices become more expensive.

When prices fall, instead of buying more, we engage in panic selling. This continual process of buy high and sell low results in the destruction of wealth.

Thus, to avoid behavioural biases in our decision-making, some investors adopt a 'passive' approach by investing in indexes such as FTSE 100, FTSE 250, which track the performance of the largest companies in the UK.

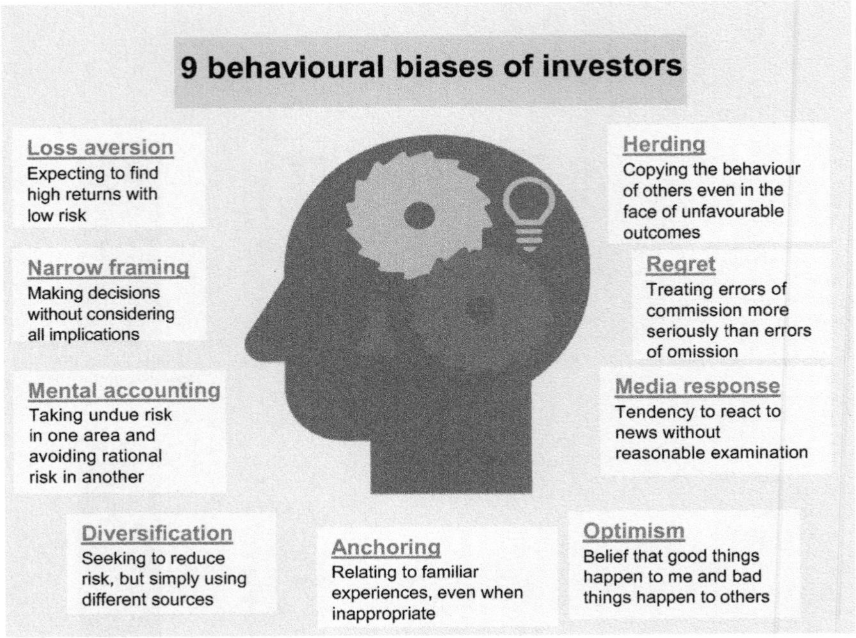

9 behavioural biases of investors

Loss aversion
Expecting to find high returns with low risk

Narrow framing
Making decisions without considering all implications

Mental accounting
Taking undue risk in one area and avoiding rational risk in another

Herding
Copying the behaviour of others even in the face of unfavourable outcomes

Regret
Treating errors of commission more seriously than errors of omission

Media response
Tendency to react to news without reasonable examination

Diversification
Seeking to reduce risk, but simply using different sources

Anchoring
Relating to familiar experiences, even when inappropriate

Optimism
Belief that good things happen to me and bad things happen to others

Figure 3.10 Behavioural biases of investors

Source: Dalbar (2015)

Table 3.8 Major causes of investor underperformance

Major causes of equity investor underperformance (20-year analysis)		
Cause	% Contributed to underperformance	Underperformance ($ bn)
Lack of availability of cash to invest	0.54	44
Need for cash (planned and unplanned)	0.68	55
Fund expenses (including management fees)	0.79	65
Voluntary investor behaviour underperformance	1.50	122
Total	**3.52**	**286**

Note: Lack of availability of cash represents the investor return that is lost by delaying the investment. Need for cash represents the percentage of investor return that is lost or gained by withdrawing the investment before the end of the period being measured.

Source: Dalbar (2016, p.10)

Figure 3.11 The cycle of investment destruction
Source: Carl Richards quoted in Roth (2014)

Ownership of property

A high proportion of households in the UK own their homes. This is good news as property prices have risen dramatically in the past decades in certain areas, and so households have seen their wealth increased. However, the percentage of ownership has fallen from its peak in 2003, with 71% owner-occupiers to 63% today.

There is also now a big generational divide, with 46% of 25–34-year-olds now living in private rentals, compared with 27% in 2006–7 (Collinson, 2018).

Besides capital growth, home ownership also means lower monthly payments on housing. Those who own their homes spend on average 18% on mortgage payments, while social renters pay 28% and those in private renting spend 35% of their income on housing, as can be seen in Table 3.9.

The number of British adults owning a second or investment property is small. Only 1 in 10 British adults own a second home. The number with multiple properties increased from 1.6 million to 5.2 million between 2000 and 2014. However, 3.4 million are not landlords, suggesting that although they own extra properties,

Table 3.9 Property ownership and renting in the UK, 2017

Types of households	Owner occupier households	Private renting	Social renting	Total
Number in millions	14.3	4.5	4	22.8
Percentage	62.90%	20%	17.10%	100%
% of income spent on mortgage payments or rent	18%	35%	28%	

Source: Jones (2017)

they are not letting these out. Instead, they leave them empty as an investment or use them as holiday home. The majority of people owning second or third properties live in the wealthiest parts of the UK – London, South East, South West and East of England (Rudgard, 2017).

Without investments in property, business or equity, the majority of British households rely on salary or paid employment as their main source of income. This earned income can be disrupted by ill health, death or redundancy.

Conclusion

Although households in the UK have financial concerns (significant increases in costs of living, worries about effects of ill health and death, insufficient money in retirement, and unexpected expenses) (Aviva, 2017a), many do not have plans in place to deal with these.

In order to achieve financial security, it is necessary to take control of your finances. This begins with mapping out your goals and objectives, building a buffer to enable you to cope with the unexpected, and taking a long-term view of your finances.

As research has shown, this requires planning for the future, controlling consumption, and actively investing.

The intangible benefits from doing these are immeasurable, giving you peace of mind and confidence to deal with whatever life brings.

References

Allen, T. and Hebner, M. (2017) 'Dalbar 2016 QAIB: investors are still their own worst enemy' [online] www.ifa.com/articles/dalbar_2016_qaib_investors_still_their_worst_enemy/.

Aviva (2017a) 'Protecting Families' [online] www.aviva.com/newsroom/public-policy-items/protecting-our-families-report-march-2017.

Aviva (2017b) 'UK: inequality worsens as savings gap grows 25% and homeownership levels fall for low income families' [online] www.aviva.com/newsroom/news-releases/2017/02/uk-inequality-worsens-as-savings-gap-grows-25-and-homeownership-levels-fall-for-low-income-families-17740/.

Bach, D. (2005) *The Automatic Millionaire*. Penguin.

Barclays (2018) *Equity Gilt Study* [online] www.scribd.com/document/383879981/Barclays-Equity-Gilt-Study-2018.

Baruwa, E. (2015) 'Health financing functions: risk pooling' [online] https://www.slideshare.net/HFGProject/risk-pooling-elaine-baruwa-final-eng.

Bellevue Community College (2008) *Personal Money Management: Fiscal Fitness for the Long Run – Get Fit!*

Brignall, M. (2017) 'Average UK debt at £8,000 per person' [online] www.theguardian.com/money/2017/oct/30/average-uk-debt-at-8000-per-person-not-including-the-mortgage.

Canfield, J. (2017) 'Visualization techniques to affirm your desired outcomes: a step-by-step guide' [online] http://jackcanfield.com/blog/visualize-and-affirm-your-desired-outcomes-a-step-by-step-guide/.

Cheema and Soman (2008) 'The effect of partitions on controlling consumption'. *Journal of Consumer Research*, 34: 665.

Clason, G. (2004) *The Richest Man in Babylon*. Signet.

Crampton, N. (2017) '20 things millionaires aren't sharing with you'. *The Entrepreneur Magazine* [online] www.entrepreneurmag.co.za/advice/personal-wealth/personal-finance/20-things-millionaires-arent-sharing-with-you/.

Collinson, P. (2018) 'UK tenants paid record £50bn in rents in 2017' [online] www. theguardian.com/money/2018/feb/12/uk-tenants-paid-record-50bn-in-rents-in-2017.

Dalbar (2016) 'Dalbar's 22nd annual quantitative analysis of investor behavior 2015 for period ended: 12/31/2015' [online] www.qidllc.com/wp-content/uploads/2016/02/2016-Dalbar-QAIB-Report.pdf.

Evolution Money (2018) 'What does a typical holiday cost?' [online] www. evolutionmoney.co.uk/help-and-advice/finance-faqs/much-people-spend-holiday.

Go Compare (2016) 'The cost of Christmas' [online] www.gocompare.com/press-office/2016/cost-of-christmas/.

The Guardian (January 2018) 'Seven in 10 UK workers are "chronically broke"' [online] www.theguardian.com/money/2018/jan/25/uk-workers-chronically-broke-study-economic-insecurity.

HMRC (2018) *UK Income Tax Liabilities Statistics: Survey of Personal Incomes with Projections to 2018–19* [online] https://assets.publishing. service.gov.uk/government/uploads/system/uploads/attachment_data/file/710866/Income_Tax_Liabilities_Statistics_May_2018.pdf.

HMRC (2017) *UK Income Tax Liabilities Statistics: Survey of Personal Incomes with Projections to 2017–18* [online] https://assets.publishing. service.gov.uk/government/uploads/system/uploads/attachment_data/file/616452/Income_Tax_Liabilities_Statistics_May_2017.pdf.

Hughes, K. (2018) '90% British people risk hardship by insuring their phones ahead of their health'. *The Independent*, 24 May [online] www.independent. co.uk/money/spend-save/uk-health-insurance-mobile-phone-insure-finances-a8366566.html.

Hull, R. (2018) 'Running a car costs £207,000 over a lifetime' [online] www.thisismoney.co.uk/money/cars/article-5414197/Average-lifetime-cost-running-car-207-000.html.

Jones, R. (2017) 'Home ownership in England at a 30-year low, official fig-ures show' [online] www.theguardian.com/money/2017/mar/02/home-ownership-in-england-at-a-30-year-low-official-figures-show.

Kirkland, G. (2017) 'How expensive are car repairs over time?' [online] www. oponeo.co.uk/tyre-article/how-expensive-are-car-repairs-over-time.

Lunn, E. (2018) 'How to meet your short and long-term saving ambitions?' (2 January) [online] www.telegraph.co.uk/money/how-to-start-saving/short-and-long-term-saving-goals/.

Millennial Finance Blog (2018) 'Personal finance 101: spend what is left after saving' [online] https://personalfinancemillennials.com/2017/07/personal-finance-101-spend-what-is-left-after-saving/.

Milligan, B. (2016) 'Millions have less than £100 in savings' [online] https://www.bbc.co.uk/news/business-37504449.

The Money Charity (2018a) 'Almost 10 m households in the UK have no savings whatever' [online] https://themoneycharity.org.uk/money-stats-almost-10m-with-no-savings/.

The Money Charity (2018b) 'The money statistics June 2018: savings and pensions' [online] https://themoneycharity.org.uk/media/June-2018.pdf.

The Money Charity (2018c) 'The money statistics September 2018' [online] https://themoneycharity.org.uk/money-statistics/.

The Money Charity (2017) 'The money statistics October 2017: savings and pensions' [online] https://themoneycharity.org.uk/media/October-2017-Money-Statistics1.pdf.

Money Magazine (2018) '4 ways to take control of your spending' [online] http://time.com/money/collection-post/3940991/control-spending-budget/.

Office of National Statistics (2017a) 'Disposable income' [online] www.ons.gov.uk/peoplepopulationandcommunity/personalandhouseholdfinances/incomeandwealth/bulletins/householddisposableincomeandinequality/financialyearending2017.

Office of National Statistics (2017b) 'Expenditure is available' [online] www.ons.gov.uk/peoplepopulationandcommunity/personaland-householdfinances/expenditure/bulletins/familyspendingintheuk/financialyearending2017.

Office of National Statistics (2016) 'Ownership of UK quoted shares' [online] www.ons.gov.uk/economy/investmentspensionsandtrusts/bulletins/ownershipofukquotedshares/2016.

Office of National Statistics (2014) 'Ownership of UK quoted shares' [online] www.ons.gov.uk/economy/investmentspensionsandtrusts/bulletins/ownershipofukquotedshares/2015-09-02.

PayPal (2018) 'Money pools' [online] www.paypal.com/uk/webapps/mpp/money-pools.

Poptech (2014) 'Money pools: a centuries-old savings tool reinvented' [online] www.csmonitor.com/World/Making-a-difference/Change-Agent/2014/0221/Money-pools-a-centuries-old-savings-tool-reinvented.

Rick, S.I., Cryder, C.E. and Loewenstein, G. (2008) 'Tightwads and spend-thrifts'. *Journal of Consumer Research*, 34: 767.

Romeo, V. (2017) 'DIY investors shun passives as advisers dominate index market' [online] www.moneymarketing.co.uk/diy-investors-shun-passive-options-advisers-dominate-index-market/.

Roth, A. (2014) 'Are you an irrational investor?' [online] https://blog.aarp.org/2014/11/17/are-you-an-irrational-investor-heres-how-to-tell/.

Rudgard, O. (2017) 'One in ten British adults now a second-home owner' [online] www.telegraph.co.uk/news/2017/08/18/one-ten-british-adults-now-second-home-owner/.

Shale-Hester, T. (2018) 'Average new car price has risen 38 per cent in the last decade, says Cap HPI' [online] http://cardealermagazine.co.uk/publish/average-new-car-price-risen-38-per-cent-last-decade-says-cap-hpi/146938.

Stanley T. and Danko, W. (2010) *The Millionaire Next Door: The Surprising Secrets of America's Wealthy*. Taylor Trade.

Tracy, B. (2018) 'Parkinson's Law' [online] www.briantracy.com/blog/financial-success/parkinsons-law/.

Young, S. (2017) 'The cost of average British wedding hits all-time high' [online] www.independent.co.uk/life-style/average-british-wedding-cost-uk-27000-hitched-venue-honeymoon-food-london-midlands-a7937551.html.

Protecting against dying too young

Lien Luu

In a nutshell:

• **Dying early could have severe financial consequences on your family.**
• **Your employer and state benefits may not be sufficient to provide financial security to your family.**
• **Life insurance has an important role in providing additional peace of mind and financial security for those you leave behind.**

Winston Churchill's powerful warning has often been used to remind us of the devastating consequences of the death of a breadwinner and underline the role of life insurance.

> If I had my way, I would write the word 'insure' upon the door of every cottage and upon the blotting book of every public man, because I am convinced, for sacrifices so small, families and estates can be protected against catastrophes which would otherwise smash them up forever.
>
> It is the duty to arrest the ghastly waste, not merely of human happiness, but national health and strength, which follows when, through the death of the breadwinner, the frail boat in which the family are embarked, founders and the women and children and the estates are left to struggle in the dark waters of a friendless world.

Life insurance has been described as 'money to deal with death's financial fallout' (Lynch, 2009). Although the proceeds are intended to tackle the financial consequences of death, interestingly these are not called death insurance, but life insurance. The reason is that life insurance is bought to provide peace of mind for the purchaser, so that their survivors have financial security in the event of their death.

Talking about death is never easy, but it is important to consider the financial consequences your surviving spouse and dependants are likely to face, so that you can do something about it now to ensure that they avoid the additional pain of financial destitution. This chapter explores the financial impact of death, the support from employer and government, and the additional cover you might need.

Why protecting your family is important

Insurance protection for loss of income in the event of illness or death is the foundation of financial security because most of your assets in the early years of your working life lie in your human capital rather than financial assets.

In the UK, the total value of human capital was estimated at £19.23 trillion in 2015, giving an average human capital of £471,000 (ONS, 2016a). Those with qualifications have higher human capital than those without qualifications. The average total value of the lifetime earnings of those with a degree or equivalent was estimated at £628,000, compared to £274,000 for those with no qualifications.

The average value of human capital in the UK is higher than the value of financial capital. The total net wealth of all households in Great Britain was £12.8 trillion (for 2014–16), giving a median household wealth of £259,400.[1] The good news is that household wealth is on an upward trend, increasing by 15% from £225,100 in 2012–14 (ONS, 2018). On average, the value of human capital is £211,600 higher than financial capital.

Many people believe that they only need to consider protection once they have acquired financial and physical assets. This proves to be a gross misconception.

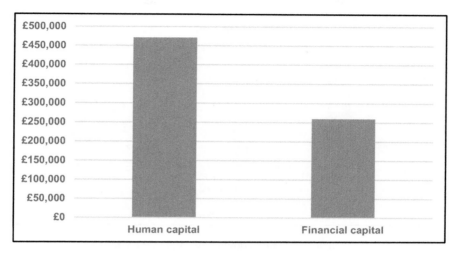

Figure 4.1 Human capital versus financial capital
Source: Author's illustration

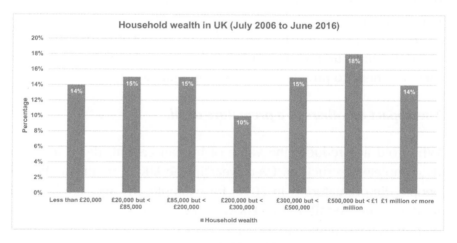

Figure 4.2a Household wealth in the UK
Source: ONS (2018)

Those who are young, for example, may have limited physical and financial assets. However, they have a higher human capital than older workers, because they have more working years and therefore more time to earn money. Similarly, those with limited financial,

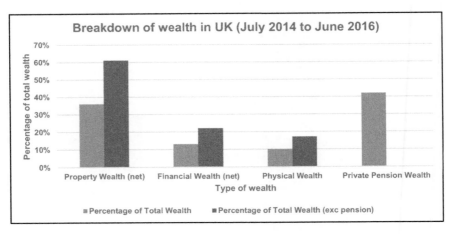

Figure 4.2b Breakdown of wealth in the UK
Source: ONS (2018)

property, physical and pension wealth will have a higher proportion in human capital.

Insurance protection is, therefore, crucial because most of your assets lie in your human capital rather than financial assets. You therefore need to protect your most important asset – you.

The impact on others of a premature death

While old age reduces the value of human capital, death leads to its complete destruction. Every year in the UK, a small number of people die prematurely. In 2016, for example, the age-standardised mortality rate (ASMR) for the UK was 982.5 deaths per 100,000 population, suggesting that there is less than 1% chance of dying young.

Mortality rates for men are higher than women: 1,128.4 deaths per 100,000 population for males (1.13%) and 838.2 for females (0.84%). The good news is that the ASMRs in 2016 decreased for both sexes, more for females (3.0%) than males (2.4%). Several factors contribute to decreasing mortality rates, including improved lifestyle, medical advances in the treatment and diagnosis of many illnesses and diseases, and government initiatives to improve health through better diet and lifestyle (ONS, 2016b and 2016c).

Jamie's story

In April 2012, Jamie, a 41-year-old IT consultant, was riding his motorcycle on his way home one Saturday afternoon. He was ten minutes away from home when a car hit him at a busy junction and he died instantly. His death shattered the lives of those he left behind: his widow and four young children aged 2, 4, 11 and 14.

Source: MK Citizen (2013)

The probability of death before the age of 65 is low (1% or less), but the impact is severe as death radically transforms the lives of those who you leave behind and profoundly affects their emotional, financial and physical well-being. Death is a difficult subject to talk about, as no one really wants to think about the inevitable. However, it is important to discuss death and plan for it because it is certain to happen but uncertain as to when and how it will occur.

I lost my dad a few years ago and that was the most painful experience I had to endure. My life was suddenly engulfed in loss and grief. While emotionally I had not come to terms with the reality that my dad had gone, I had the painful task of registering the death, organising the funeral, and breaking the news to our relatives. I was not able to focus on work for a few months, and luckily my employer was sympathetic and allowed me to take time off work.

Symptoms of grief include anxiety, sleep problems, lack of concentration, mood swings and tearfulness, numbness, and a sense of isolation.

The process of bereavement may follow four phases (Fisher Center for Alzheimer's Research Foundation, 2018):

- Shock and numbness: Family members find it difficult to believe the death; they feel stunned and numb.
- Yearning and searching: Survivors experience separation, anxiety and cannot accept the reality of the loss. They try to find and bring

back the lost person and feel ongoing frustration and disappoint-
ment when this is not possible.

- Disorganization and despair: Family members feel depressed and find it difficult to plan for the future. They are easily distracted and have difficulty concentrating and focusing.
- Reorganisation: Survivors begin to accept their loss and establish new ties with others, with a gradual return of interests and activities.

The intensity, duration and expression of grief varies from individual to individual, depending on age, gender, history of loss, the relationship's nature and quality, social networks, religion and culture
(Lynch, 2009, p.32).

While the death of a parent is hard to deal with, the death of a
spouse, who may have been the main breadwinner, might inflict
additional pain. You might lose a confidante, a source of income and
a shoulder to rely on, and have to take on new roles left by his or her
departure. In *A Grief Observed*, C.S. Lewis reflects on bereavement
and describes his experiences following his wife's death. He recounts
the 'mad midnight moments' of his mourning and elucidates the
questions, doubts and anger brought on by his sorrow. He explains
the difficulties of coping with everyday life without his wife and the
pain that comes with the realisation that what he wants most he can
never have again (Lynch, p.33).

In addition to emotional pain, death might also cause money worries, as survivors have to deal with a permanent loss of income and
lifetime earnings. Imagine a family loses a 35-year-old breadwinner
on a salary of £40,000 per year. The death would result in a permanent loss of £40,000 per year for the next 30 years.

The loss of income has several consequences. First, it might push
the family below the poverty line. Research shows that the overall
drop in income following the death of a partner pushes one in five
households (20%) below the official poverty line (Corden, Hirst and
Nice, 2008, p.79).

The same research also shows that women are more likely than men
to be financially worse off after the death of a partner, irrespective of

the loss of any particular income stream (Corden, Hirst and Nice, p.83). More women than men are likely to face economic hardship because many are poorly placed to take up jobs that replace lost earnings, due to caring responsibilities. Women with dependant children may struggle initially to take up or return to paid employment after their partner dies. The study concludes that death of a partner is one cause of family and child poverty (Corden, Hirst and Nice, p.151).

Household income may also be affected because surviving partners may find it difficult to stay in their jobs. Research by the University of York shows that people who had gone back to work but then left their jobs or went on sick leave, pointed to the following contributory factors:

- Having poor health since bereavement
- Going back to work too early after the shock of sudden death
- Development of additional stress, related to work (Corden, Hirst and Nice, p.77).

While losing an income, death creates additional expenses, such as funeral, **probate** (confirmation in Scotland) and estate settlement costs, and inheritance taxes for larger estates, and these have to be paid quickly.

According to a report by Royal London, the average cost of a basic funeral in the UK in 2015 was £3,700, but the total cost was £6,000 if extra expenses such as flowers, a reception and a headstone are included (Grant, 2015). By 2016, *The Telegraph* reports that the average funeral cost in the UK was £3,897 (cremations), but the total cost of dying was £8,802 to include costs for the send-off and professional administration of the estate (*The Telegraph*, 2017). However, burials are more expensive, costing almost £5,500 on average (up by more than a quarter in five years), and if other costs are included, the total cost is much higher (Chapman, 2017).

The surge in funeral costs have resulted in 'debt poverty' as families who struggle with funeral costs take on debt. In 2017, the average debt taken on by bereaved families who struggled to pay was £1,680 (Royal London, 2017).

For those who cannot pay the funeral costs, the council will pay for a 'pauper's funeral', or a 'public health funeral'. It is estimated that 4,000 people in the UK are buried or cremated this way every year, costing local authorities an estimated £4 million. In this type of funeral, family members might not be allowed to attend the service and the ashes might not be returned to the family. The deceased is buried or cremated with no gravestone or lasting physical memorial - just an unmarked grave (*Independent*, 2018; Wyatt and Strangwayes-Booth 2015).

Some families might struggle to make ends meet due to insufficient income. Some may even lose their homes if they cannot afford to pay mortgage payments. Research by the University of York shows that one of the most pressing financial issues immediately after the death of a partner is whether they are safe in their home. Many attach deep emotional significance to the property and most want to stay on. Those who own their home and have paid off their mortgage have no fear, but for those who have not paid off their mortgage or are in rented accommodation, there is uncertainty about their future (Corden, Hirst and Nice, p.107).

Finally, survivors face additional stress as they may have to take on new roles within family and domestic life: greater responsibilities for child care, household management, shopping and cooking, money management and driving. Taking on these new roles is often stressful, with anxieties, frustrations and disappointments (Corden, Hirst and Nice, p.140).

Marion's story

In 2010 Geoffrey died at the age of 55, leaving behind his wife Marion and their three sons all under 17. Geoffrey had a joint life insurance policy of £100,000 but the mortgage was £500,000. Marion, working part-time, was not able to keep up with the mortgage payments, and was forced to sell the family home to pay off the loan. Fortunately, the family could move into one of their buy-to-let properties, but it wasn't as comfortable as their own home and they had the upheaval of having to move. Geoffrey didn't take out enough life insurance because he couldn't 'afford it'.

Life insurance usually focuses on survivors' financial needs. However, it can also perform a powerful role in the transition for survivors by giving them the necessary time to grieve and adjust. As one author has shown, although life insurance cannot prevent or end grieving, hopefully it can provide the time and resources to enable grieving survivors to focus on dealing with their loss by allowing them to take time off work and relieving financial stresses (Lynch, p.33).

Financial impact of death

Biggest worries in the event of death:

- Impact on family's wellbeing 49%
- Family not being financially protected 34%
- Impact on those financially dependent 22%

Source: Legal & General, 'Deadline to breadline' (2017)

How can you protect your family against the financial impact of death?

You can help alleviate the financial impact of death on your family in two ways – **self-insure** or transfer the risk to a **life assurance** company.

The main benefit of taking up a life insurance policy is that the policyholders have immediate access to a capital value (i.e. the sum assured) from day one. This is a clear advantage over **precautionary saving** which requires time to build up the required savings/capital, and exposes individuals to insufficient funds in the meantime (Mahdzan and Diacon, 2008).

Let's imagine that an individual takes out a life insurance policy with a sum assured of £200,000. If they die at any time within the term of the policy, the family would receive a payment of £200,000 from day one.

It would take 20 years to build up a sum of £200,000, requiring a saving of £10,000 per year or £833 per month, an unrealistic sum for many. In the UK, households save on average £105 per month and so it would take 160 years to save £200,000. If you have a large debt, insurance is essential.

The role of life insurance

Life insurance is important because it enables your survivors to pay off debts. Taking out a life insurance policy requires many decisions at the start of the policy. There are many issues to consider: who needs to be insured; how much cover; how long is the term; what type of policy (**term insurance** or **whole of life insurance**); should the policy be single or joint; and which insurance provider to choose.

The most important decision is deciding how much cover to buy and for how long. This will depend on several needs, as shown in Figure 4.3.

- Capital needs: this is the amount needed to pay off a mortgage and any other loans, specific legacies, and any inheritance tax liability.
- Short-term capital needs: the amount required to pay for funeral expenses and other debts.
- Income needs: this is the amount of replacement income your survivors require to maintain their lifestyle.

A rough rule of thumb is that a working parent should insure a lump sum amount worth between five and ten times their

Figure 4.3 Factors to take into account in life insurance purchase
Source: Author's diagram

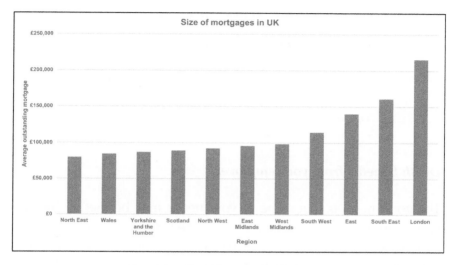

Figure 4.4 Size of mortgages in the UK
Source: Boyce (2016)

annual salary to meet the family's income needs. For example, for someone with a salary of £20,000, a £200,000 life insurance is recommended.

In reality, the amount of life insurance needed depends on the amount of borrowing outstanding and the living costs of the survivors, both of which can vary depending on where they live. As the biggest debt is usually mortgage loan, those in London and the South East will probably need a higher amount of life insurance. Funeral costs are also more expensive in the capital.

To calculate how much life insurance you might need, you might want to use a life insurance calculator.

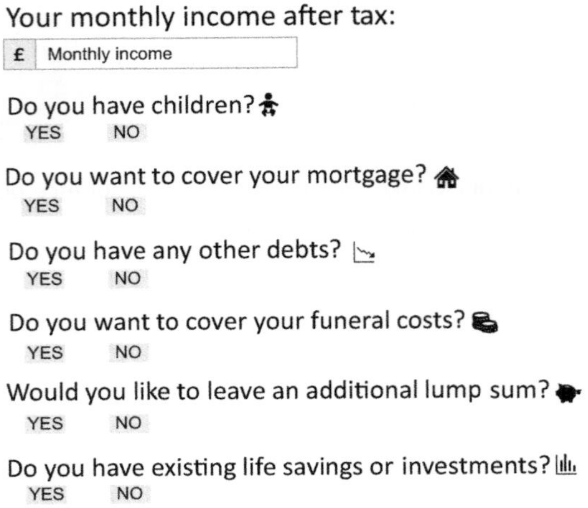

Your monthly income after tax:

£	Monthly income

Do you have children? 🧍
YES   NO

Do you want to cover your mortgage? 🏠
YES   NO

Do you have any other debts? 📉
YES   NO

Do you want to cover your funeral costs? 💰
YES   NO

Would you like to leave an additional lump sum? 🪙
YES   NO

Do you have existing life savings or investments? 📊
YES   NO

Figure 4.5 Factors determining amount of life insurance
Source: L&G (2018)

Death benefits from your employer

The good news is that some of your needs may be met by benefits you get from work. Many employers in the UK provide life and health benefits to their employees. In 2016, 10.9 million members belonged to group life, income protection and critical illness schemes. The most significant benefit provided by employers is life insurance, known as death in service. In 2016, 8.3 million people were members of group life schemes and thus were provided with death-in-service benefit (ABI, 2018a, p.32).

Activity: Employee benefits checklist

Do you really know what your employee benefits are?

1. How much life cover does your employer provide? This is often called death-in-service benefit.

2. Does your life cover or death-in-service lump sum pay off the mortgage or leave enough for your loved ones to keep their home long term?
3. What other savings or money can your family get hold of if you or your partner dies?

The level of life insurance on offer at work varies considerably, from zero to 14 times yearly salary. In research conducted for *HR Magazine*, Punter Southall Health & Protection Consulting (PSHPC) surveyed more than 400 of its corporate clients that together employ over 110,000 employees.

The report found great discrepancies in death-in-service benefits. The financial services industry topped PSHPC's table, providing life cover of an average of 4.63 times yearly salary. For a mid-level manager on, say, £50,000 a year, this works out at a lump sum of £231,500 on death – nearly a quarter of a million pounds, entirely tax-free.

Within the financial sector, one in 16 schemes (6%) provides life cover of seven or more times salary. For top managers and directors earning, say, £200,000 a year, such schemes could pay a lump sum of £1.4 million or more.

PSHPC's survey discovered one financial firm offering life cover 14 times the salary. For someone earning £50,000, this would produce a pay-out of £700,000 (D'Arcy, 2015).

The survey above shows that people working in highly paid sectors, such as banking and IT, also receive the most generous financial benefits on top of their high wages.

Public sector workers such as nurses, doctors and police officers appear to receive a lower death-in-service lump sum benefit than those who work in the above sectors. In the UK, 5.424 million people (or 17% of the 31.95 million working) work in the public sector

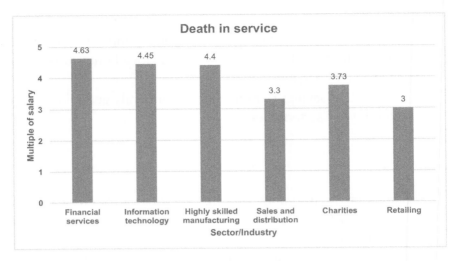

Figure 4.6 Death in service by sector
Source: D'Arcy (2015)

(ONS, 2017). Their death-in-service benefit is an amount equivalent to between 1–3 times salary but does usually come with more generous survivors' pensions compared to the private sector (Silverliningep, 2017).

The report also found that not all employers offer this valuable protection to their workers, and that sectors and industries without a strong history of unionised labour provide their workers the lowest levels of life insurance. This is demonstrated by the case of Pennie.

Pennie's story

Pennie worked for a supermarket in Blackfield, near Southampton. She had five children aged between 14 and 20 and died in 2015. She earned £12,000 and was the sole earner. On her death, her children received four weeks' basic salary of £1,100, compared with the estimated £36,000 to £48,000 that many other high street retailers would have paid out as a death-in-service benefit if Pennie had been working for them and been earning the same salary.

Source: Jones (2015)

Death in service and tax

For higher earners, the payment of death in service could have tax implications. The *Financial Times* reports that millions of higher earners risk leaving loved ones with unexpected tax bills as a result of death-in-service payments (Cumbo, 2017). There are three reasons for this.

First, it is not widely known that death-in-service benefits are typically paid as a lump sum under a pension scheme. This means the payment could trigger a **lifetime allowance charge** if the worker had built up substantial pension rights and savings before their death. The charge is triggered if the total value of private pension benefits, including death benefits exceeds £1.03 million (in 2018–19; and this limit increases each year in line with inflation). Although that sounds a lot, pensions can be very valuable – your pension scheme at work can tell you the value of your workplace pension and you'll need to add in the value of any other pensions you have.

Second, a death in service payment is sometimes paid into the estate of the deceased rather than direct to the survivor. This means, if the deceased's estate is high enough, there may be inheritance tax to pay or, in the case of married couples, there may be a higher inheritance tax bill when the survivor eventually dies – see the box for why this can happen. Yet, in this situation, inheritance tax is easily avoided. If you have a death-in-service benefit, your employer will usually ask you to nominate somebody to receive it if you die. It is vitally important that you complete this form. The death-in-service scheme will be looked after by one or more trustees. They have discretion to decide who will receive the benefit when an employee dies. Although they are not obliged to follow the wishes you have set out on the nomination form, in the vast majority of cases they will. And, because the payment is at their discretion, the benefit goes direct to your heirs, bypassing your estate, and so no inheritance tax is involved. However, if you have not completed the nomination form and it is not clear who should receive the benefit, it will be paid to your estate and so could trigger or increase an inheritance tax bill.

Third, where the nomination form is completed, the vast majority of people nominate their husband or wife. While this ensures no inheritance tax is paid on the death of the employee, it will swell the estate of the surviving spouse and could mean extra inheritance tax when he or she eventually dies (see the box). A solution would be, instead of nominating your spouse, use the form to ask for the benefit to be paid into a **trust** – sometimes called a 'spousal bypass trust'. The potential beneficiaries of this trust can be the surviving spouse and children or grandchildren. That means that the survivor can have use of the assets in the trust but usually by borrowing anything they need; on their death, the money has to be paid back before inheritance tax is calculated, so their estate does not increase at all (Silverliningep, 2017). This is a complex area, so you should obtain expert advice from a solicitor (for example, a member of the Society of Tax and Estate Practitioners*) or financial adviser* skilled in this area.

Inheritance tax and couples

Inheritance tax is mainly a tax on the estate you leave when you die. However, some bequests are tax-free, in particular anything you leave to your husband, wife or civil partner – but not an unmarried partner. In addition, regardless of marital status, the first slice of each person's estate is tax-free as follows:

- Nil-rate band: the first £325,000 of any assets.
- Main residence nil-rate band: a further £125,000 (in 2018–19, rising in stages to £175,000 by 2020–1) which applies to a home you pass on to your direct descendants (chil-

dren, grandchildren, and so on). However, this is tapered away to nothing for estates worth more than £2 million.

Anything above the tax-free part is normally taxed at a rate of 40%.

Married couples and civil partners often leave their estates to each other. Since these bequests are tax-free, there is a special rule to prevent the nil-rate bands being wasted. This allows a surviving married or civil partner to inherit any unused part of the nil-rate bands of the first of the couple to die. So when the survivor eventually dies, there may be up to £650,000 of nil-rate band and up to a further £250,000 of main residence nil-rate band (in 2018–19) to set against their estate. Surviving unmarried partners cannot inherit their deceased partner's nil-rate bands and so cannot pool their estates tax efficiently in this way.

Support from the government

The government also offers some benefits to support surviving husbands, wives and civil partners in the event of death in the form of **bereavement benefits** – but, again, not to unmarried couples. However, a radical change, introduced in 2017, restricts the amount of benefits available. Under the new scheme, instead of receiving support until the youngest child leaves school – maximum 20 years – parents will receive support for just 18 months. The changes are expected to save the government £100 million a year, but it is estimated to affect as many as 6,000 of the 8,500 families expected to claim in 2018 who will be significantly *worse* off. From 2017, parents with children are believed to be anywhere from £6,000 to £12,000 a year worse off, at a time when they're unable to work to support their child (Munbodh, 2017).

Figure 4.7 shows the amount of **bereavement support payment** paid from April 2018 where a spouse or civil partner died on or after 6 April 2017.

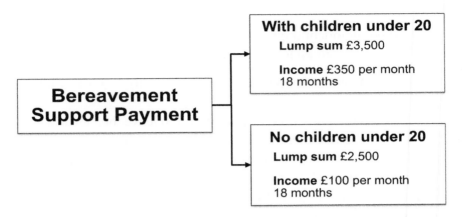

Figure 4.7 State bereavement benefits for surviving spouses and civil partners

Source: Author's chart

Although the government provides some support, many people will need to take out additional private cover to ensure that their loved ones can maintain their living standard.

Anil's story

Anil and Rehana lived with their two young children in rented accommodation, with Rehana staying at home to look after the children. The family were managing financially. Though they had a loan, they could comfortably afford the repayments.

Rehana died from a sudden illness, leaving behind Anil and their two young children.

After Rehana's death things were not so easy financially. Anil understandably wanted to spend more time with his young children and help them through the difficult time, but he was also the main breadwinner and couldn't afford for the family income to drop. The children needed to be looked after and by either reducing his hours or sending them to nursery there was a financial cost to be incurred.

A charity stepped in to help the family financially so Anil could reduce his working hours and spend more time with his children while they all go through this very difficult time. Anil wants to be there for his children but he too needs emotional support and time to heal from Rehana's death.

Amanda's story

Richard died from cancer leaving behind Amanda and their two children, one of whom has learning difficulties and the other has been diagnosed with an on-going illness. Added to this Amanda has now been diagnosed with a long-term illness that has meant considerable time off work for treatment.

A charity has been helping the family with payments for necessary purchases for several years now. Amanda has tried incredibly hard to be self-sufficient but with her illness it became extremely hard to make ends meet and pay for additional costs such as travel to and from hospital and hospital parking. Small amounts that soon add up to large amounts especially when the household income is already stretched so tightly.

Source: The Insurance Charities (names have been changed) (2018)

What are the different life insurance policies available?

Your employer and the government provide some help but many people may need to 'top up' the benefits by taking out a life insurance policy. In the UK, there are three main types of life insurance – **lump sum term assurance**, whole of life and **family income benefit**.

A lump sum term assurance contract is relatively cheap because it provides coverage for a limited period, normally set up to age 65, and a single lump sum amount is paid only if death occurs in this period.

Term insurance provides pure insurance coverage because nothing is paid if you do not die during the term of your life insurance policy. In the UK, many policies are set to expire at the age 65 but on average people live to the age of 80. This means that few term life insurance policies are paid out, and thus the cost is relatively low.

It is difficult to establish the number of households with a term life insurance policy. According to the ABI, 0.5 million of 27.2 million households (1.8%) had term life insurance in 2016 (ABI, 2018a), but 5 million, or over 18%, had a whole of life policy (ABI, 2018a). To this figure, we need to add 8.3 million members who receive life insurance cover (or death in service) from work (ABI, 2018b, p.32), giving a total of 13.8 million. This total is close to the figure reported by the *Independent*. This states that about a quarter of people in the UK (14 million) had life insurance in 2018, but that number had fallen by 3.6 million from 2017 (Hughes, 2018).

A whole of life policy tends to be more expensive than term life insurance because there are two elements to the policy: investment and insurance.

The policy has no expiry date (but is renewable every 5–10 years), and the policy pays out a lump sum if death occurs. As the policy has an investment element, it might have a value when the policyholder decides to cancel the policy, while a term life assurance has no cash-in value if the policy is cancelled. A whole of life policy is normally used to pay an anticipated inheritance tax.

While a term or a whole of life policy pays out a lump sum to pay off the mortgage, survivors often have no income to live on, as is illustrated in Anil and Amanda's stories. The survivor receives a lump sum from an insurance policy to pay off mortgage and other **liabilities**, but has no income to live on. He or she and the children are potentially forced to live in relative poverty.

Ingrid's story

Fifty-year-old Hugo died in a car crash. He had a life insurance policy for £200,000. His widow Ingrid received a lump sum insurance pay-out, enabling her to buy a bigger house in a better area.

They had four children. Working part-time as a nurse earning £20,000 a year, Ingrid found it difficult to support the children. In the end, she had to sell the big house.

A family income benefit policy is therefore designed to address this problem of a lack of a replacement income in the event of the death of a wage earner. A term life insurance policy provides a lump sum to pay off a mortgage, while a family income benefit policy pays an income to survivors. A family income benefit policy is also known as a decreasing term policy because as each year passes, the number of years of pay-out is reduced.

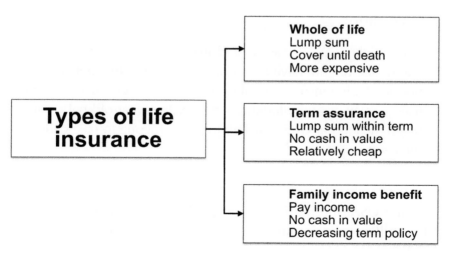

Figure 4.8 Types of life insurance

Source: Author's chart

Why people don't buy life insurance

Aviva estimates that only 46% of families with dependent children in the UK have life insurance. If this is the case, then 54% of families with children have no life cover. Indeed, it is estimated that more than 8.5 million families have no life insurance in the UK (Rutt, 2016).

The life insurance gap

The life insurance gap, in the UK and globally, is huge. Swiss Re put the global life insurance gap in 2013 at US$86 trillion, or 116% of the world's GDP. For the UK, Swiss Re estimated that the gap was £2.4 trillion in 2006. It appears that £4.2 trillion worth of cover was needed to pay for the expenses of all UK families (including mortgage payments and basic family expenses), but only £1.8 trillion protection cover was in place. By 2011, the protection gap in the UK had risen to about US$4 trillion, or £2.6 trillion. Experts believe that the low uptake of life insurance is due to the fact that many families see it as an additional and unnecessary expense (Schanz and Wang, 2014).

Guy's story

Thirty-eight-year-old Sasha died from breast cancer. Unfortunately, she did not have life insurance as it was thought she did not need a life insurance policy as she was a housewife. Sasha used to stay at home looking after her two-year-old baby. Her death meant that Guy now had to pay someone to take care of their son.

In the USA, the life insurance gap is also massive, estimated at $15.3 trillion as many Americans do not have life insurance (Schanz and Wang).

According to research, the most common reason given by people who do not have insurance is that they have competing financial priorities. The second most common reason is that they think they cannot afford it. Yet, it is reported that 70% of US households with children under 18 would have trouble meeting everyday living expenses within a few months if a primary wage earner were to die today. Four in ten households with children under 18 say they would immediately have trouble meeting everyday living expenses.

Behavioural biases

Individuals in the UK, and indeed across the globe, are grossly under-insured. There are fundamental reasons why people do not buy, or buy enough, insurance.

In the UK, a Deloitte report found that the reasons why people are not buying life insurance include unclear benefits, complexity, lengthy application process, and other competing financial priorities. The report also observes a clear disconnect between prospective buyers' views on short-term financial goals and priorities and the potential longer-term financial benefits associated with purchasing life insurance (Deloitte, 2015, p.9).

These behaviours manifest deeper biases. One is *loss aversion*. People do not value future benefits as much as they feel the pain of paying for the cost now.

Kunreuther (1996) demonstrated that people usually fail to insure themselves against 'low probability, high loss' risks, even when the terms and premiums are favourable. The 'loss' of premium is seen to outweigh the 'gain' of any insurance recovery because the premium loss is exaggerated.

For example, an individual pays £30 per month for a life policy for a sum assured of £100,000. Loss aversion means that the loss of premium of £30 per month causes more pain than the potential gain of £100,000 in the event of a claim. The pain arises partly because an insurance policy promises a future benefit (one may never materialize), while premiums are a current cost.

They are also affected by the concept of availability – the ability to conceptualise and relate to the risks if they have not experienced any loss.

A study conducted in California by Kunreuther (1996) found that before an earthquake in 1989, 34% of uninsured homeowners thought earthquake insurance as unnecessary. After the tragedy, only about 5% gave the same response and one-third of the previously uninsured homeowners decided to insure their properties against earthquake.

This concept of *availability* helps explain the low demand for life insurance: individuals do not buy insurance because they do not think it is necessary as they cannot relate to the risk and may believe that things will take care of themselves.

Conclusion

Death can shake the lives of the survivors, both emotionally and financially. Though not an easy topic to discuss, having a plan to deal with the consequences of death is necessary so that financial destitution and distress can be avoided.

Survivors need time to grieve and mourn the loss of a loved one. The absence of financial pressures and money worries might enable them to cope better in times of grief. Fortunately, there are simple solutions available.

Your greatest asset lies in your human capital and this is insurable. You can transfer the risk and worries to an insurance company, in return for peace of mind and financial protection for your loved ones. Pure life assurance policies are relatively cheap and should be considered essential if you have people who will be affected financially by your death. Indeed, they deserve your love and compassion, not the risk of poverty, when the inevitable happens.

Note

1   Total wealth includes property wealth, financial, physical, and pension wealth. If pension wealth is excluded, the median household wealth was £156,000 (ONS, 2018).

References

ABI (2018a) 'UK insurance and long term savings: key facts 2018' [online] www.abi.org.uk/globalassets/files/publications/public/key-facts/abi-key-facts-2017.pdf.

ABI (2018b) 'UK Insurance and Long term Savings: State of the market', available at www.abi.org.uk/globalassets/files/publications/public/data/abi_bro4467_state_of_market_v10.pdf.

BBC News (2015) 'Paupers' funeral costs rise by 30% in five years' [online] www.bbc.co.uk/news/uk-wales-34963133.

Boyce, L. (2016) 'The regions with the biggest mortgage debt revealed' [online] www.thisismoney.co.uk/money/mortgageshome/article-3438660/The-regions-biggest-mortgage-debt-revealed-Use-interactive-maps-town-city-compares.html.

Chapman, B. (2017) 'Families forced into 'death poverty' and debt as funeral costs surge to £5,500', available at www.independent.co.uk/news/business/news/uk-families-death-poverty-funeral-costs-debt-bill-estate-inheritance-tax-5500-a7727536.html.

Corden, A., Hirst, M. and Nice, K. (2008) 'Financial implications of death of a partner'. University of York, December, Working Paper Number ESRC 2288, 12.08 [online] https://www.york.ac.uk/inst/spru/research/pdf/Bereavement.pdf.

Cumbo, J. (2017) 'Millions at risk of death in service shock' [online] www.ft.com/content/d77788c4-0b38-11e7-ac5a-903b21361b43.

D'Arcy, C. (2015) 'How much life insurance does your job pay?' [online] www.lovemoney.com/news/19941/death-in-service-life-insurance-job.

Deloitte (2015) *Life Insurance Consumer Purchase Behaviour: Tailoring Consumer Engagement for Today's Middle Market*, September [online] https://www2.deloitte.com/content/dam/Deloitte/us/Documents/strategy/us-cons-life-insurance-consumer-study.pdf.

Fisher Center for Alzheimer's Research Foundation (2018) 'Bereavement and grief' [online] www.alzinfo.org/articles/bereavement-and-grief/.

Grant, P. (2015) 'Cost of a funeral soars to £3,700 – but what do you get?' [online] www.bbc.co.uk/news/business-34424586.

Hughes, K. (2018) '90% British people risk hardship by insuring their phones ahead of their health' *Independent*, 24 May [online] www.independent.co.uk/money/spend-save/uk-health-insurance-mobile-phone-insure-finances-a8366566.html.

Independent (2018) 'Poorest families "being barred from funerals of relatives" because they can't afford to pay for them: council tells loved ones they are not allowed to attend or have ashes if they cannot pay for a service' [online] www.independent.co.uk/news/uk/home-news/funerals-barred-paupers-poorest-families-bracknell-forest-council-a8371496.html.

The Insurance Charities (2018) In-house case studies [online] www.theinsurancecharities.org.uk.

Jones, R. (2015) 'Death in service: how much should employers pay out when tragedy strikes' [online] www.theguardian.com/money/2015/jan/24/death-in-service-how-much-should-employers-pay.

Kunreuther, H. (1996) 'Mitigating disaster losses through insurance' [online] http://opim.wharton.upenn.edu/risk/downloads/archive/arch167.pdf.

Legal & General (2017) 'Deadline to breadline' [online] www.legaland-generalgroup.com/media-centre/press-releases/uk-employees-just-one-month-from-the-breadline-new-research-by-legal-general-reveals/.

Legal & General (2018) *Life Insurance Calculator* [online] www.legaland-general.com/life-cover/confused-about-life-cover/life-insurance-cover-calculator/.

Lynch, J.T. (2009) 'The unspoken need for life insurance'. *Journal of Financial Service Professionals*, March: 32–3.

Mahdzan, N.M. and Diacon, S. (2008) 'Protection insurance and financial well-being'. December, [online] www.researchgate.net/publication/275209568_Protection_Insurance_and_Financial_Wellbeing.

MK Citizen (2013) 'School governor escapes jail term' [online] www.miltonkeynes.co.uk/news/school-governor-escapes-jail-term-1-4760947.

Munbodh, E. (2017) 'Grieving families to be £12,000 worse off under new bereavement benefits' [online] www.mirror.co.uk/money/bereavement-benefits-grieving-families-worse-10038674.

Office of National Statistics (2016a) 'Human capital estimates 2014 to 2015' [online] www.ons.gov.uk/peoplepopulationandcommunity/wellbeing/articles/humancapitalestimates/2015.

Office of National Statistics (2016b) 'Deaths registered in England and Wales, 2016' [online] www.ons.gov.uk/peoplepopulationandcommunity/birthsdeathsandmarriages/deaths/bulletins/deathsregistrationsummarytables/2016.

Office of National Statistics (2016c) 'Deaths registered by usual area of residence' [online] https://www.ons.gov.uk/peoplepopulationandcommunity/birthsdeathsandmarriages/deaths/datasets/deathsregisteredbyareaofusual residenceenglandandwales.

Office of National Statistics (2017) 'Public sector employment, UK: June 2017' [online] www.ons.gov.uk/employmentandlabourmarket/peopleinwork/public sectorpersonnel/bulletins/publicsectoremployment/june2017.

Office of National Statistics (2018) 'Wealth in Great Britain wave 5: 2014 to 2016' [online] www.ons.gov.uk/releases/wealthingreatbritainwave 52014to2016.

Royal London (2017) 'A false dawn: funeral costs rise again after one year respite', p.20 [online] www.royallondon.com/Documents/PDFs/2017/ Royal-London-National-Funeral-Cost-Index-2017.pdf.

Rutt, R. (2016) 'One in four breadwinners don't have life insurance leaving their families with a cover gap of £263 billion' [online] www.thisismoney. co.uk/money/news/article-3387027/One-four-UK-breadwinners-not-life-insurance-buy-life-cover.html.

Schanz, K. and Wang, S. (2014) 'The global insurance protection gap assessment and recommendations: a Geneva Association research report' [online] www.genevaassociation.org/sites/default/files/research-topics-document-type/pdf_public/ga2014-the_global_insurance_protection_gap_1.pdf.

Silverliningep (2017) 'Why the taxman likes death in service benefits' [online] www.silverliningep.co.uk/why-taxman-likes-death-in-service-benefits/.

The Telegraph (2017) 'How much does a funeral cost by region' [online] www.telegraph.co.uk/financial-services/retirement-solutions/funeral-plans/average-cost-funerals-uk/.Wyatt, C. and Strangwayes-Booth, A. (2015) 'Paupers' funerals cost councils £1.7m' [online] www.bbc.co.uk/ news/uk-34943805.

Protecting your income

Lien Luu

In a nutshell:

- **Your ability to work is dependant on your health.**
- **Your health can be insured against illness, disability and incapacity.**
- **State benefits are not adequate to maintain your standard of living.**

Imagine that you had a money printing machine that every month tirelessly went about its task, printing money for you and your family five days a week.

If this is your sole source of income, what would you do to ensure that the printer does not stop printing?

- Service it and keep it in tip top condition
- Ensure that it is insured against temporary breakages
- Cover it for total breakage, if you are unable to ever fix it again

If you are employed, you are that money-printing machine. The printer epitomises your capital (skills, knowledge and experience), and the functioning of the machine symbolises your health and your ability to work. As your income is predicated on your health and your ability to go to work, it is fragile because of the risk of illness and disability. If you are unable to get up and go to work each day, the flow of your income will be disrupted.

The good news is that there are a range of benefits that may be available through your job, including **statutory sick pay**, employer's own **sick pay** scheme, group income protection provided by employer, early retirement through ill health in case of permanent disability and access to private medical insurance which can help get you back to work quickly. However, depending on your circumstances, you may need to consider topping up these benefits to ensure that you can maintain your current lifestyle.

Experts generally agree that protecting your income is vitally important. It is difficult to establish with accuracy the number of households in the UK with an income protection policy. While Aviva calculates that around 8% of adults in the UK have income protection (Aviva, 2017a), the ABI reported that 11.8% of the 27.2 million households in the UK in 2015–16 may have had income protection, with 1,185,000 holding an individual income protection policy, 2,016,000 a group income protection policy and 570,000 a group critical illness policy (ABI, 2018).

Income protection is not very well known or understood. The Aviva 2017 report, for example, found that 40% of parents in the UK do not think they ever need or want income protection. Yet, income protection is the most important tool they have against long-term disability. Also known as **permanent health insurance**, income protection provides income replacement in the event of ill health. By providing a tax-free replacement income of 50–70% of income for a period of up to 52 years for a policy taken out at age 18, an income protection policy gives you the means to maintain your lifestyle and the time to focus on recovery.

Income protection pays out for an extended period of time. It has been aptly described as a wealth preservation tool, as in the event of long-term disability you will receive payments from an insurance company rather than deplete your savings. As Mark's story shows, income protection can provide financial security for the old and the young alike.

As only a small proportion of UK households have income protection, the income protection gap is enormous. Swiss Re estimated that the income protection gap in the UK amounted to £175 billion of annual benefit in 2015. By 2017, this gap rose to an estimated £200 billion and the total estimated 'protection gap' in the UK was £2.4 trillion (Mahdzan and Diacon, 2008 and Contractor Weekly, 2017).

Mark and Beryl's story

In his 20s, Mark had a great career lying ahead of him as a trainee accountant. He was also looking forward to buying a house with his girlfriend.

One afternoon after work, he crossed a busy road and was hit by a truck. This left him paralysed from the waist down. This tragedy not only resulted in the breakup of the relationship, his mother, Beryl, also had to give up her job to look after him. Without a replacement income, Mark was condemned to a life of financial destitution.

On a global scale, the percentage of people with income protection varies considerably. Hong Kong and Malaysia (62% and 63% respectively) have the highest proportion with insurance against serious illness/disability, and Germany and the UK have the lowest (17% and 20%, respectively) (Zurich, 2016, Global survey findings, p.4). There is a strong correlation between knowledge and purchase of insurance and it is therefore not surprising that people in Hong Kong and Malaysia are more knowledgeable about serious illness and disability insurance: 50% and 59%, respectively, in comparison with 14% and 19% in Germany and the UK who have 'good to very good knowledge'.

The same survey also shows the varying degree of willingness to spend on income protection. Malaysians, Mexicans and Hong Kong Chinese are prepared to spend the most on income protection (more

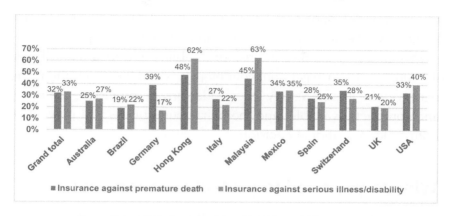

Figure 5.1a Global ownership of health and life insurance
Source: Zurich (2016)

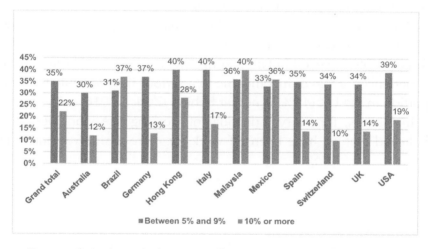

Figure 5.1b Percentage of income willing to spend on income protection
Source: Zurich (2016)

than 10% of income), while Australians are the least willing. In the UK, 14% are willing to spend more than 10% of income on income protection and 34% between 5–9%. The report concludes that many respondents over-estimate the cost and that income protection is available for less than 5% of earnings (though individual costs vary by age and level of protection). Perception of the cost may be a factor in the low take up of income protection (Zurich, 2016, pp.7–10).

This chapter examines the risk of disability and long-term illness, the support you may get from your employer and the government, the reasons why it is necessary to consider private provision, the insurance products available, and the behavioural biases that prevent us from making a rational decision.

Why do you need to protect your income?

Poor health is a major risk that we all face. It is generally accepted that the risk of being off work due to illness or accident is much higher than the risk of premature death.

Zurich Global Survey (2016) shows that many people worldwide experience a loss of income due to a serious illness. Half of the respondents surveyed in Hong Kong, Mexico, Spain and Brazil have experienced a loss of income due to a serious illness, while the proportion in the UK (42%) is not far behind (Zurich 2016, p.7).

In the UK, for every individual of working age who dies, it is believed that 14 have been off work for more than six months. In

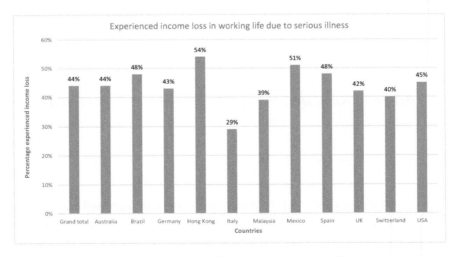

Figure 5.2 Experience of losing income due to illness

Source: Zurich (2016)

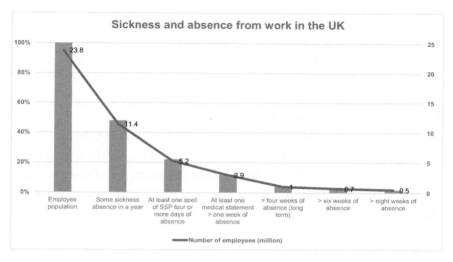

Figure 5.3 Incidence of sickness absence (employees only)

Source: Black and Frost (2011, p.86)

the UK, around 2.2 million people of working age are economically inactive due to ill health (ABI, 2014, p.11).

The Black and Frost 'Health at work review' (2011) found that 140 million working days are lost every year in the UK due to sickness absence, equivalent to 2.2% of working time, costing employers £9 billion every year.

Most of the sickness is short term, but each year more than one million workers are off sick long term (for more than a year) because of medical problems (Kyriakou, 2017).

In addition, around 250,000 people (1% of the workforce) leave employment each year due to ill health. More than half of these people (60%) are the main household earner and so their inability to work has a significant financial impact.

What are the consequences of ill health?

If you cannot work for more than a year, how do you think you and your family will cope?

A report by Aviva in March 2017 shows that 57% of families would struggle if they lose a source of income permanently. In the UK, many households do not have an adequate safety net and so will experience a drop in income and consequently living standards. Indeed, the Money Advice Service reports that 21 million UK adults did not have £500 of savings in 2017 (Kyriakou, 2017).

In a report published in September 2014, research commissioned by the ABI shows that 10.8 million middle-income households in the UK would be entitled to little or no state support if the principal earner could not work. Of these households, 6.6 million would see their income drop by 50% if the principal left work due to ill-health (ABI, 2014, pp.7, 10).

Aviva also revealed the effects of ill health on the families involved in its report in August 2017:

- Nearly one in three (31%) UK adults has experienced leave from work due to unexpected ill health, a cancer diagnosis or even a death in the family.
- Of these, 77% or 12.3 million people have seen their finances suffer as a result.
- They have seen their income drop by a quarter (24%) and savings and investments fall by two-fifths (40%).

Table 5.1 How well do parents expect they would cope if the following affected the main income earner (in %)?

	Temporary loss of income due to ill health for at least 6 months	Long term loss of income due to ill health for at least 12 months	Permanent loss of income due to ill health	Permanent loss of an income due to death
Expect they would cope well	50	37	30	38
Expect they would not cope well	40	52	57	47

Source: Aviva (2017a, p.10)

- Two in five (38%) had to apply for benefits or other government support while 22% had to use their savings.
- One in six (15%) had to downsize, move in with family, rent or in extreme cases even became homeless.
- 1.9 million people who have experienced an unexpected illness or death don't think they'll ever financially recover (Aviva, 2017b).

In short, then, with the advent of disability or illness, income drops drastically while expenses rise. In the UK, there are some state benefits but there is still a gap between the amount received in benefits and expenditure. A private insurance policy (e.g. income protection) provides a replacement income and narrows the gap between income and expenditure.

Besides financial repercussions, long-term illness also precipitates other problems. One is known as 'social drift', when sufferers move house to a cheaper area. Children move to new schools; family treats and holidays are a thing of the past.

They are also likely to suffer medical conditions that affect their mortality. The family also may suffer more illness. It has been suggested that the effects of long-term unemployment could have the same effect on health as smoking ten cigarettes a day (Walker, 2010, p.31).

Illness and disability are also likely to lead to increased debts. According to the Citizens Advice Bureau, illness and disability was the third major reason for debt problems given by their clients in 2008. In some cases, the debt had arisen because clients had to give up work due to their own ill health. In other cases, the client had to give up work to care for an ill or disabled relative. While income drops, expenditure may rise because they need to keep the heating on for longer or require a special, more expensive diet (ABI, 2014, p.14).

Financial difficulties unsurprisingly create intense stress and over the years have contributed to an increase in the numbers of people experiencing mental illness. It is estimated that each year 1 in 6 workers in England and Wales is affected by anxiety, depression and unmanageable stress. An OECD report published in 2014 reveals that each year mental ill health costs the UK economy £70 billion, or 4.5% of GDP, through lost productivity, social benefits and health-care costs. Mental disorders are believed to account for 38% of **disability benefit** claims (ABI, 2014, p.14).

Macmillan Cancer Support's 'Hidden price tag' survey

This survey, published April 2013, shows that:

- 4 out of 5 cancer patients were hit by the financial cost of cancer, which averaged about £570 a month. This is comparable to the average monthly cost of a mortgage.
- 85% of cancer patients experienced extra expenditure costs, averaging around £270 a month. Typical extra costs included travel to and from medical appointments, appointment parking costs, treatment prescription costs, home help or live-in support.
- 54% of cancer patients experienced higher day-to-day living costs as a result of their diagnosis (e.g. higher fuel bills as they spend more time at home), which cost them on average £63 a month.
- 47% of cancer patients' financial situations get worse after diagnosis.

Source: ABI (2014, p.13)

Help from the government and employers

In the UK, when people are off sick, there is some state benefit available. If an employee leaves work due to health or disability, employers are required to pay statutory sick pay (SSP) for up to 28 weeks (six months) for just under £90 per week (£390 per month). Some employers (43%) offer some form of sick pay over and above minimum statutory requirements in the form of **occupational sick pay** (OSP).

When SSP ends, an employee can then apply for state welfare benefits (**employment and support allowance** ESA) provided that they have paid **National Insurance** for at least two years. ESA is initially paid for 13 weeks during which applicants go through a **work capability assessment** to determine their eligibility.

The Carol Black and David Frost 'Health at work review' estimated that around 110,000 people each year move from SSP or OSP to claiming ESA and a further 140,000 moving straight from employment to claiming ESA (ABI, 2014, p.8).

Although there is some sick pay benefit provided in the UK, there are three fundamental issues.

First, employees receive sick pay for a maximum period of 28 weeks (just over six months).

Second, the amount of £90 per week is well below the average UK household spending of £528 per week – in fact, the payment constitutes only 17% of the average national spending (ONS, 2017).

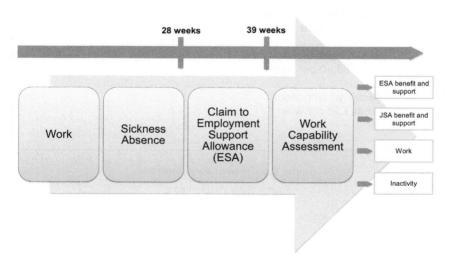

Figure 5.4 The journey through occupational and state support

Source: ABI (2014, p.8)

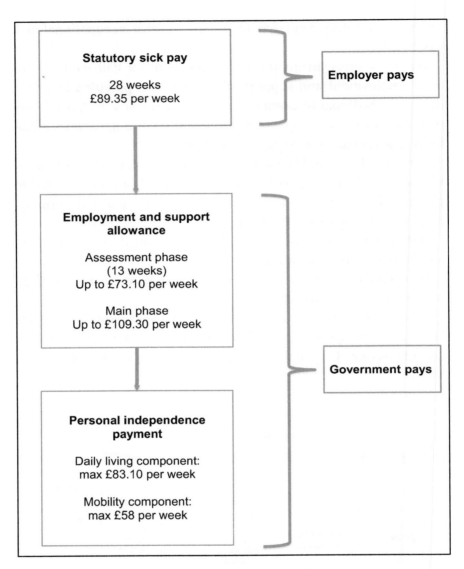

Figure 5.5 Types of state benefits

Source: Author's own chart

There is thus a big shortfall between what you might need and what you receive.

Third, when the SSP payment ends, eligibility to sick pay is means tested and entitlement unclear.

The UK welfare system has been criticised because it is based on 'a fundamentally flawed assumption that households [who] get little or no support from the state recognise this and act to put in place their own safety net' (ABI, 2014, p.4).

Households then need a system that will give them a clearer understanding of:

1. How much income support they can get from the state if they have to stop work due to ill health
2. How much income support they will get from their employer
3. How they can top up their income safety net to the level they need (ABI, 2014, pp.4, 9).

The self-employed in the UK fare a lot worse as they are not entitled to statutory sick pay. Though they can claim ESA, their eligibility is not guaranteed and this is means-tested.

How do you respond to a loss of income due to ill health?

Aviva's 2017 'Protecting families' report shows some interesting actions on how families intend to cope with a loss of income due to ill health. These include cut back on monthly spending, apply for government support, sit tight and see how things develop, cash in on savings and investments, and sell personal possessions.

Some of the proposed actions may not be practical or can meet financial needs. For example, Aviva's report shows that households need a minimum of £1,904 per month to live on (Aviva, 2017a, p.12). So, even if families receive state benefit, there is a sizeable shortfall of £1,500 per month.

Table 5.2 How parents would respond to a loss of income due to ill health for a period of at least six months (in %)

	First step	Second measure	Last resort	Never
Cut back on monthly spending	53	20	12	5
Apply for government support i.e. state benefits	30	23	24	7
Sit tight and see how things develop	26	24	19	15
Cash in on savings and investments to provide extra money	16	26	21	7
Sell personal possessions	13	27	31	10
Ask parents for financial support	9	19	29	16
Move to a cheaper rented property	6	12	24	23
Access my pension savings as soon as I can, regardless of whether I have retired	6	13	25	18
Ask another family member for financial support	5	12	27	28
Sell the house and move to a smaller/ cheaper one	5	13	34	16
Look to borrow money from a high street lender (e.g. credit card, overdraft, personal loan)	5	14	28	35
Ask siblings for financial support	4	12	25	28
Sell the house and rent instead	3	8	24	28
Sell the house and move back in with family	3	7	20	30
Look to borrow money from a non-high street lender (e.g. payday loan, doorstep lender)	3	7	16	54

Source: Aviva (2017a, p.14)

What do you need to do to protect yourself and your family?

Sick pay from your employer and the government goes some way to help but you might need to take out a private policy to cater for your needs and take into account your circumstances. For example, you might need a longer period of time to recover and a higher amount of income to meet your expenses. An individual policy can be tailored to meet your lifestyle needs.

There are three possible courses of action you can take to provide financial security for you and your family: 1) precautionary saving, 2) insurance policy or 3) alternative sources of income.

Precautionary saving

Precautionary saving is more flexible than an insurance policy. However, the risk of poverty or depletion of wealth is high when the illness is prolonged. In addition, given the low savings in the UK, many households do not have a sufficient buffer.

> **Activity**: To determine how long your savings can support you, think of the savings you have and the amount you spend every month. Then, on Figure 5.6, sketch a line showing how much you have set aside in savings (vertical axis) and how long you think that amount would support you (horizontal axis) if your income from work stopped.

Insurance policies

In the UK, there are three different types of insurance you might consider for income protection:

- **Accident, sickness and unemployment (ASU) insurance**: this is a short-term policy, providing cover for up to two years. The benefit is normally a fixed sum not related to earnings. Policies, such as **mortgage payment protection insurance** (MPPI), are a form of ASU that is designed to cover just the costs of the mortgage and sometimes certain household bills, but not living costs generally.

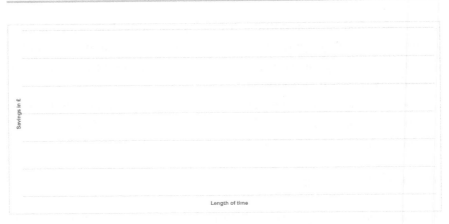

Figure 5.6 How long might your savings support you?
Source: Author's template

- **Critical illness cover** pays a one-off lump sum or an income. This can be combined with life insurance or stand-alone. A critical illness policy often requires 30 days survival before pay-out. Death before 30 days often results in non-payment. It is therefore often recommended to combine critical illness with life insurance. The lump sum can be used to pay off debts, or pay for treatments (e.g. speech therapy) and adjustments to the home (e.g. wheelchair access). A critical illness policy with life insurance pays out just once on diagnosis of, say, cancer. The money might be needed to spend on treatment. This means that dependants are no longer protected against the event of death. If you have dependants, it might worthwhile to consider a 'buy back option'. This allows you to continue to have life cover after a critical illness claim by paying an extra premium.

    It is estimated that 9% of individuals in the UK have a critical illness policy, in comparison to 12% who have phone insurance. Yet, the risk of developing a critical illness is real. In 2017, 3.5 million people were diagnosed with a critical illness (Hughes, 2018).
- **Income protection policy** (also known as permanent health insurance): this is designed to provide cover for long-term disability as

it provides payment until the insured gets better or retired. Potentially, cover is provided for a period of more than 52 years (if the policy is taken out at 18). Income protection insurance allows the insured to protect a large percentage of their income – up to 50–70 per cent – which is paid out tax-free. Income protection is good for high earners as it provides cover based on *income*, rather than *expenses* (in contrast to, say, MPPI).

Dibyesh's story

Dibyesh, in his late 40s, suffered a heart attack and survived. He had a critical illness policy and received a lump sum. This enabled him to pay off the mortgage and allowed him to take a less stressful job after his recovery. He thought critical illness insurance was the best thing he had.

Ed's story

Ed, a 50-year-old man, suffered a stroke. Although he recovered, he lost his speech and is now taking speech therapy. He worked for a small firm and unfortunately did not have critical illness cover or income protection. Luckily, his wife earned a good salary.

Income protection and critical illness policies are complimentary rather than alternatives, as one provides an income and the other a lump sum. Where budget is an issue, income protection is recommended because it covers more conditions (mental illnesses and back trouble) than critical illness.

Figure 5.8 lists some of the reasons for income protection claims, including progressive illness (cancer), mental illness or depression, musculoskeletal problems, heart, blood pressure or blood circulation

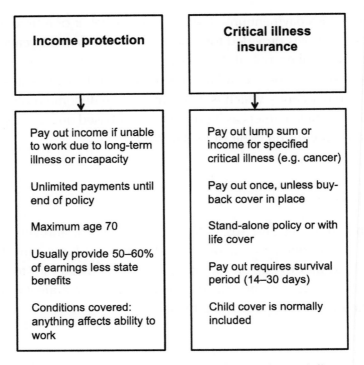

Figure 5.7 Differences between income protection and critical illness cover
Source: Author's chart

problems, stomach, liver, kidney or digestive problems, and chest or breathing problems. An interesting feature is the high number of claims due to mental illness or depression (ABI, 2014, pp.4, 9).

Alternative sources of income

You can also protect yourself against the financial impact of long-term incapacity by setting up residual or passive income. It is generally recognised that there are two types of income: **active income** (also known as earned income, or linear income) and **residual income** or recurring income. While active income relies on your ability to go to work, residual income can operate independently and does not depend on you. This means that if you cannot work due to health reasons, your income is not being affected.

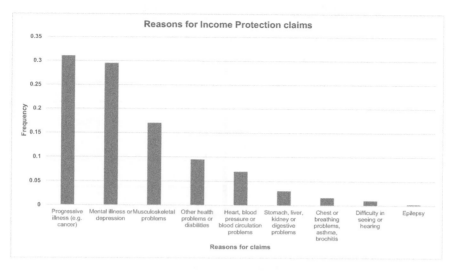

Figure 5.8 Reasons for income protection claims
Source: ABI (2014, p.9)

Some of the world's richest people become rich due to residual income. Writers, for example, receive royalties from their books. They write a book once, and then they can sell an *unlimited* number of copies *indefinitely* if there is demand. Musicians also receive royalties from their music. They record a song once and every time their song is played, they receive money. What is also powerful is that this income is still paid to them (or their family) after their death. Michael Jackson's estate, for example, has received more than $1 billion since his death. Fans mourned his tragic death around the world, resulting in more than 415,000 albums sold in the first four days in America alone – and 2.3 million songs downloaded across the world (Murray, 2010).

After her death, Whitney Houston's estate has also received royalties from her songs and, in 2012 alone, took in an estimated $10 million. Unlike Jackson who co-wrote and owned most of his music, Houston's estate received much less from royalties because she did not write or own her songs. The bulk of royalties go to the songwriter and the publisher, who get about eight cents every time

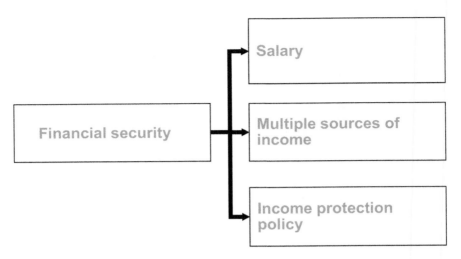

Figure 5.9 Strategies to achieve financial security
Source: Author's chart

one of their songs is played on the radio. Houston's famous song 'I Will Always Love You' was written by Dolly Parton in 1973 and so she earns a royalty every time this song is played (Tracy, 2012).

Residual income can come from many other sources including renting out investment properties, and receiving dividends from shares, interest from savings, and income from a traditional or internet business.

In the UK, some people have sought to build a source of residual income by investing in **buy-to-let** properties. In the UK, the buy-to-let market has experienced a massive growth. *The Telegraph* reported in October 2014 that there were 2 million landlords in the UK owning 4.9 million properties worth nearly £1 trillion. It was predicted that buy-to-let properties would increase by another 1 million in five years (Dyson, 2014).

The recent changes (higher taxes on rental income, extra stamp duty for second property, stricter affordability rules) have put a brake on the rapid expansion of the buy-to-let market. The number of landlords has remained relatively stable, and in February 2018 the *Guardian* reported that there were still around two million landlords owning more than five million properties.

However, the biggest change is to the income they receive. The *Guardian* reported that in 2017 tenants paid £51.6 billion in rents, an increase of £1.8 billion on the previous year and more than twice the £22.6 billion in 2007. The average rental income earned by a buy-to-let landlord is around £20,000 a year (though the averages are skewed by a small number of landlords who own a large portfolio of properties) (Collinson, 2018).

Let's imagine that you have a buy-to-let property which gives you a gross monthly profit of £500 before tax. How many properties do you need to give you a lifestyle you want?

Besides property investment, you can take advantage of the internet to make money, for example, by selling ebooks, writing a blog, or setting up a YouTube channel. Many people sell ebooks on Amazon and, once an ebook is created, it produces a source of residual income. Some people use ghost writers, as in the case of Saeed Rajan of *Escape Your Desk Job*, who is reported to make around $2,700 a month by publishing ebooks on Amazon, and he hasn't written a word himself (Assadi, 2018). Elance and Freelancer provide access to writers who can take care of the writing while Fiverr.com can help with logos and design front cover of the book. Creating a passive income now gets easier and easier. All you need is an idea.

Why people don't buy income protection: behavioural biases

Perceived value

Many people do not buy income protection because they simply do not think that they will need it, as after all statistically only 1% of people become incapacitated each year. For others who consider the impact and consequences of ill health, the cost of income protection is too high. Aviva's 'Protecting families' report finds that parents are more likely to insure their physical possessions than their health or income, with perceived affordability found to be the most common barrier (Aviva, 2017a, p.3).

Top five products where affordability is a preceived issue among parents without cover (%)			
	I think I should have this, but I haven't yet	I don't think I can afford this	I don't think that I will ever need or want this
Health insurance (including dental)	14	41	39
Life insurance	27	37	30
Critical illness cover	20	37	36
Long term care plan	21	35	35
Income protection cover	18	35	40

Figure 5.10 Top five products where affordability is a perceived issue among parents without cover

Source: Aviva (2017a, p.8)

A lack of awareness

A lack of awareness may also explain the low take up of income protection. Many people believe they do not need income protection. Aviva's survey reveals that 40% of parents do not think they will ever need or want income protection and only 18% think they should have it. Greater awareness of the features and benefits of income protection therefore is essential.

Families in the UK may also overestimate their ability to cope. A Zurich report shows that 63% respondents in the UK believe they have savings to cover more than six months in the event of serious illness and disability, and 23% can survive for one month (Zurich, 2016, p.8).

However, Legal & General's 'Deadline to breadline' shows that households have a much lower level of financial resilience. The report examines the number of days on average UK employees and their households could survive financially on their savings if income is lost through long-term sickness, critical illness or death. This shows that UK employees can survive 32 days (or one month) and 23% could be on the breadline tomorrow as they do not have savings (Legal & General, 2018).

The CII's report 'Building resilient households' also confirms that many UK households cannot rely on their savings if they lose their income for a long period. It shows that almost half (46%) of UK

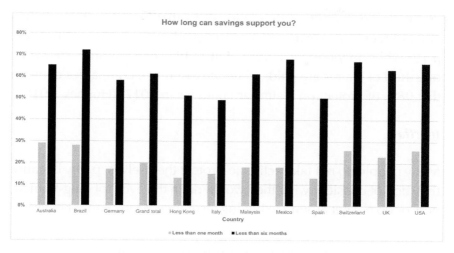

Figure 5.11 How long can savings support you?
Source: Zurich (2016)

households have savings of less than £1,500. A quarter (25%) of Britons could only afford to pay household bills for a maximum of three months if they or their partner were unable to work due to long-term illness, and just over a quarter (26%) could only make a maximum of three monthly mortgage payments (CII, 'Building Resilient Households', 2016).

The benefits of income protection need to be conveyed more clearly.

Complexity

Income protection is a complex product. The complex interaction between income protection and state welfare support means that it is not clear to consumers how much replacement income they are buying and how much net income they will have as a result of the insurance.

Trust

A lack of trust also compounds the problem. While consumers believe that somewhere between 38% and 50% of income protection claims are paid, life insurance companies stress that in reality 91% of individual income protection claims are paid (as in 2013) (ABI, 2014, p.19). The *Independent* reports that public perception is that only one third of claims are paid, while life insurance companies contend that 98% of protection claims are paid (as in 2017) (Hughes, 2018).

Inertia

Many people do not take action to protect themselves, partly because they do not consider what they would do in the event of long-term illness or do not get around to buying insurance. Many cannot envisage

Table 5.3 Top concerns of parents with children

Top ten concerns of parents with dependant *children*			
Concerns	All parents (%)	Parents in low-income families (%)	All UK adults (%)
Significant increase in the price of basic necessities (e.g. food or utilities)	45	59	40
Me or a member of my family developing a serious illness or condition	43	53	43
Insufficient money for retirement	43	52	34
Unexpected expenses (e.g. major repairs to home, car costs)	42	48	33
The impact of Brexit and/or government changes	36	35	35
Losing my/our jobs (e.g. due to ill-health or redundancy)	33	42	31
Identity/cyber fraud	30	36	32
Low interest rates on savings	29	30	35
Loss of/changes to the current benefits system	29	52	26
Not being able to afford to buy a house/keep up with mortgage repayments	27	34	21

Source: Aviva (2017a, p.5)

themselves being sick for any length of time; many believe that the state will provide if they are; and some believe they have sufficient collateral to tide them over.

Indeed, Aviva finds that 76% of parents have no financial plan to deal with lost income due to ill health (ABI, 2014, p.19, Aviva, 2017a, p.1). Indeed, the same report shows that many parents have other priorities, such as significant increase in the price of basic necessities, and that ill health may be a less pressing concern.

Conclusion

Employers and the government offer various types of benefits to help you cope in the event of ill health. It is important to understand what these benefits are, how much they offer, and how long these are paid. If these are not sufficient to allow you to maintain the lifestyle you have been accustomed to, it might be necessary to consider private provision.

Experts generally agree that income protection is probably the most important protection product to buy, because it gives you a source of income if you are unable to work in the event of disability or long-term illness. If you have low or no savings, an income protection policy is critical, while for those who have savings, an income protection policy can act as a wealth preservation tool.

Private provision, whether it is an income protection policy or an alternative source of income, should act as a pillar of your financial security, ensuring a continuous flow of income when your health prevents you from working and earning a living.

References

ABI (2018) 'UK insurance and long term savings: key facts 2018', pp.4, 15, 23 [online] www.abi.org.uk/globalassets/files/publications/public/key-facts/abi-key-facts-2017.pdf.

ABI (2014) 'Welfare reform for the 21st century: the role of income protection insurance', available at www.abi.org.uk/globalassets/sitecore/files/

documents/publications/public/2014/protection/welfare-reform-for-the-21st-century.pdf.

Assadi, A. (2018) 'How to make money ($2,700/month) publishing Amazon Kindle eBooks with no writing – passive income case study' [online] www.armanassadi.com/passive-income-publishing-ebooks.

Aviva (2017a) 'Protecting families', March, available www.aviva.com/newsroom/public-policy-items/protecting-our-families-report-march-2017.

Aviva (2017b) '12 million UK adults suffer financial hardship due to unexpected ill health', 18 August, available at www.aviva.com/newsroom/news-releases/2017/08/12-million-uk-adults-suffer-financial-hardship-due-to-unexpected-ill-health-or-death-17814/.

Black, C. and Frost, D. (2011) Health at Work – An Independent Review of Sickness Absence [online] https://assets.publishing.service.gov.uk/government/uploads/system/uploads/attachment_data/file/181060/health-at-work.pdf.

CII (2016) 'Building resilient households: the future of financial provision for those too ill to work' [online] www.cii.co.uk/media/7292361/cii_building_resilient_households_report_28oct2016.pdf.

Collinson, P. (2018) 'UK tenants paid record £50 billion in rents in 2017'. Guardian, 12 February [online] www.theguardian.com/money/2018/feb/12/uk-tenants-paid-record-50bn-in-rents-in-2017.

Contractor Weekly (2017) 'The UK's £2.4 trillion protection gap' [online] www.contractorweekly.com/insurance-news/uks-2-4-trillion-protection-gap/.

Dyson, R. (2014) 'Buy to let boom: one in five homes now owned by landlords'. The Telegraph, 22 October [online] at www.telegraph.co.uk/finance/personalfinance/investing/buy-to-let/11179073/Buy-to-let-boom-one-in-five-homes-now-owned-by-landlords.html.

Freelibrary (2018) 'Report says Britons less inclined to buy health insurance' [online] www.thefreelibrary.com/Report+says+Britons+less+inclined+to+buy+health+insurance.-a0540680469.

Hughes, K. (2018) '90% British people risk hardship by insuring their phones ahead of their health' Independent, 24 May [online] www.independent.co.uk/money/spend-save/uk-health-insurance-mobile-phone-insure-finances-a8366566.html.

Kyriakou, S. (2017) 'The need for income protection'. Financial Times, 5 January [online] www.ftadviser.com/protection/2017/01/05/need-for-income-protection/.

Legal & General (2018) 'Deadline to breadline', available at www.legalandgeneral.com/adviser/protection/news-and-insight/deadline-to-breadline/.

Legal & General (2014) 'Deadline to the breadline report 2014: on the brink' [online] www.legalandgeneralgroup.com/assets/portal/files/pdf_182.pdf.

Mahdzan, N.M. and Diacon, S. (2008) 'Protection insurance and financial well-being'. December [online] www.researchgate.net/publication/275209568_Protection_Insurance_and_Financial_Wellbeing.

Murray, R. (2010) 'Michael Jackson Royalties Up 70%' [online] www.clashmusic.com/news/michael-jackson-royalties-up-70.

Office of National Statistics (2017) 'Family spending in the UK: financial year ending March 2016' [online] www.ons.gov.uk/peoplepopulation-andcommunity/personalandhouseholdfinances/expenditure/bulletins/familyspendingintheuk/financialyearendingmarch2016#uk-households-spent-more-than-4500-a-week-on-restaurants-and-hotels-for-the-first-time-in-5-years.

Tracy, B. (2012) 'Whitney Houston's financial worth after death'. CBS News, 17 February [online] www.cbsnews.com/news/whitney-houstons-financial-worth-after-death/.

Walker, C. (2010) 'Don't overlook income protection'. *Professional Adviser*, 25(3): 31.

Zurich (2016) Global survey findings, 'Income protection gaps: challenge and opportunity', p.4 [online] www.zurich.com/_/media/dbe/corporate/knowledge/docs/income-protection-gaps-challenge-and-opportunity-june-2016.pdf.

Love your workplace pension

Jonquil Lowe

In a nutshell:

- **In your 20s, 30s or 40s? You still need to think about life after work.**
- **State and workplace pensions are the key to saving enough.**
- **In your 50s or older? Be wary about cashing in your pensions.**

If you're under 50 and about to skip this chapter, stop! Before you decide, try the quiz below. If you're already 50 or over, I'm guessing you have a lot of questions about pensions, so read on.

Know yourself quiz

1. Suppose you take some faulty goods back to a local shop for a refund of £300. The shopkeeper is about to close for the day and, although willing to give you the £300 now, offers you £330 if you would not mind waiting until tomorrow. What do you do?
2. Imagine you already have £10,000 savings set aside for the long-term, half invested in shares and half in a savings account. Based on whatever you know about current investment conditions would you change the proportion invested in shares?

---

3. If you had an unexpected £500 bonus from work, what would you be most likely to do? Spend it or save it?

4. Imagine you have done some freelance work for a big firm and your invoice for £1,000 requests payment within 30 days, with a penalty of £100 if the firm pays late. Which would you prefer: £1,000 in 30 days' time or £1,100 in 31 days?

5. Imagine you have inherited £20,000 in cash and decide to invest it for the long term, splitting it between a savings account and shares traded on the **stock market**. Based on whatever you know about investment conditions today, roughly how much you would invest in shares?

Experts (for example, see Kahneman, 2011) say we avoid mental effort whenever we can. Instead of analysing our options, we use mental shortcuts. But this introduces behavioural biases that can prevent us making good decisions. If you answered 'spend it' at Question 3 in the quiz, you might be inclined to a behavioural bias called **myopia** (short-sightedness). It means you're at risk of putting off decisions until it's too late. If, at Question 1, you decided you'd rather have your money today but, at Question 4, you thought waiting an extra day was better, you're displaying **present bias**. This suggests that later on you're likely to regret decisions that you take (or fail to take) today. Finally, if you chose to stick with the existing balance of savings and shares at Question 2, but at Question 5 put a different amount in shares, you may be prone to **status quo bias** – a tendency, when faced with a choice, to stick with the current situation rather than make a decision.

If these behavioural biases apply to you, you need to read this chapter.

Retirement saving basics

Why even spring chickens need to plan ahead

The bad news about retirement is that it's expensive, so you need to start planning for it as early as you can. The good news is that, for most employees, your employer helps with saving for retirement.

If you're 50-plus, you may already be starting to panic about retirement or alternatively anticipating what you'll do with that lovely pot of pension savings once you can get your hands on it from your mid-50s onwards. This chapter will help you think through your options.

How much retirement income will you need?

Surveys (NEST, 2014; Centre for Research in Social Policy, 2018) suggest that a single person needs at least £15,000 a year (around half of UK average earnings) to get by in retirement. (Couples would need less than twice that, assuming they share some living costs.)

You might hope for more and a common rule of thumb is to aim for a pension equal to a half or two-thirds of your pre-retirement pay. For example, if you currently earn £30,000, you might aim for between £15,000 (half) and £20,000 (two-thirds).

As Ian in the case study below suggests, having enough is not just about your standard of living – it's also about feeling in control of your life.

Ian's story

'It was a struggle when the help with **council tax** suddenly stopped', says Ian. 'I had to makes cuts elsewhere but I get by'. Ian has a very small workplace pension on top of his **state pension**. He has a few hundred pounds in savings and owns his own home but still has a mortgage (taken out to buy out his wife's share when they divorced years ago). State benefits used to help with both council tax and interest on the mortgage. But help with council tax was cut back and the **mortgage interest support** is being replaced with a loan from the state to be paid off when Ian's home is eventually sold. 'I wish I'd saved more when I worked', reflects Ian. 'It's not so much the money itself. But it would be nice to feel in control instead of worrying about what the government might do to me next'.

Where will your retirement income come from?

The main source of most people's retirement income is the pensions that they have built up while working. There are three main sources: the state; your workplace; and your own 'personal' pension savings.

These days, most employees are **automatically enrolled** into a pension scheme at work. You can opt out if you like, but since your employer must pay something towards your pension, opting out of the workplace pension scheme is like turning down part of your pay packet. The government also helps towards the cost by:

- Adding to the amount you pay in – for example, if you pay in £80, the government adds £20, taking the total to £100. (The amount the government adds is called 'tax relief'. Depending on the type of scheme, tax relief may be given in a different way and, if your earnings are high, you may be able to claim extra relief.)
- Letting pension savings grow tax-free.
- Letting you have back up to a quarter of your savings tax-free, when you're ready to start drawing them out. (You pay income tax on the rest.)

When will you retire?

People are living longer. As a result, the age at which you can start receiving your state pension is increasing. Using the chart below, find your approximate date of birth on the horizontal axis and run your eye up to the line for women or men to find your **state pension age** on the vertical axis. For example, I was born in May 1957 and can see from the chart that my state pension age is going to be 66.

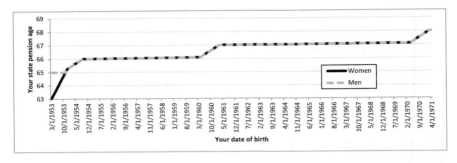

Figure 6.1 Your state pension age

Source: Author's chart based on data from: HMSO, 2007, section 13; HMSO, 2011, section 1; HMSO, 2014, Part 3; DWP, 2017

At present, the latest state pension age – which (subject to government confirmation) is expected to apply if you were born after 5 April 1971 – is age 68, but this might rise further in future.

State pension age for women born before 6 November 1953 is lower than that for men but, for people born from then on, men and women get their state pension from the same age.

A lot of workplace pensions start to be paid at the same age as the men's state pension age. You can often start it earlier, but then the pension you get will be lower for the rest of your life.

Many people opt to carry on working – maybe part-time or self-employed – even after their pension starts.

Action points: You can ask for a statement of how much state pension you've built up so far from the Pension Service*. With most workplace and personal pensions, you'll automatically get a statement each year.

It's rare these days to have one job for life, so by the time you retire you may have built up pensions with several employers and in a variety of different schemes. As you move jobs, it's easy to lose track of old pensions. There is a government service, the Pension Tracing Service*, that can help you track down lost pensions.

How to build up your savings

Make a plan

To make sure you can retire when you decide and on the level of income you want, you need a plan of action. Your plan should have these elements:

- Your goal: how much retirement income do you want and when do you want it to start?
- Your resources so far: how much retirement income are you already on track to get?
- Action to plug any gap: what can you do if you're currently not on track for your retirement goal? You essentially have three options (which you can mix and match): save extra, retire later, retire on a lower income.
- Regular reviews: to check that you are on track and make changes if not.

Figure 6.2 provides an example of what a plan might look like.

My goal: retirement income	From age 68	£18,000 a year
Resources: pensions I'm already on track for:		
State	£8,300 a year	
Work (current employer)	£3,200 a year	
Previous employer scheme	Say £1,500 a year	
Total pensions so far		£13,000
Gap to fill		£5,000
Action	Look at saving more	

Figure 6.2 Example of a plan for saving for retirement

Source: Author's example

How much should you save?

There's a common rule of thumb that says, for a comfortable retirement, you should: 'halve your age and start to save'. So if you're 30, save 15% (half of 30) of your income; if you're 50, you should save 25%, and so on. As pensions have become more expensive, a variant is: halve your age and add 7. So at age 30 you'd save 22% (15 + 7) of your income.

Like many rules of thumb, these ones are rough and ready and don't necessarily work for you personally. But they highlight that saving for retirement means setting aside a substantial chunk of money. In many workplace schemes, the maximum going into your pension is increasing in stages to reach 8% of your pay – with your employer and the government paying half and you paying the other 4% (TPR, nda). This is not even 8% of your total pay, but pay between a lower and upper limit. In 2018–19, these limits are £6,032 and £46,350 (TPR, ndb). This level of saving is probably not going to be enough for the retirement you want, so you may want to look at saving extra.

How much extra?

In Table 6.1, I've suggested how much you might need to start saving today to produce an extra £1,000 a year of retirement income. I've adjusted the sums for inflation, so that the pension you'd end up with should be enough to buy the same as a sum of £1,000 would buy today.

I've had to make some assumptions about how the future will pan out – they're explained in the note under the table. It's inevitable that the assumptions won't be exactly right – after all, nobody has a crystal ball! But they are a reasonable starting point. You'll need to review the progress of your savings regularly to see if your savings are doing better or worse than I've assumed. You can then tweak your plan accordingly.

Rebekah and Arif in the case studies below demonstrate how you can use the table. But the key points to note are that the amount you need to save each month is smaller if:

Table 6.1 Amount you might need to save each month to generate an extra £1,000 a year of pension

Later you start retirement: age at start										
	70	£27	£32	£38	£46	£58	£76	£105	£165	£344
	69	£28	£33	£40	£48	£61	£79	£110	£173	£360
	68	£29	£35	£41	£50	£63	£83	£115	£180	£376
	67	£30	£36	£43	£52	£65	£85	£119	£186	£388
	66	£31	£36	£44	£53	£67	£87	£121	£190	£396
	65	£32	£37	£45	£54	£68	£89	£124	£195	£406
		45	40	35	30	25	20	15	10	5
		Earlier you start to save: years until you retire								

Source: Author's calculations, using annuity rates from MAS (2018)

Notes: The numbers are based on these assumptions: tax relief at basic rate of 20% added to monthly amounts shown; price inflation averages 2.5% a year; earnings increase in line with price inflation; invested contributions grow by 5% a year before charges; charges are 0.75% a year; pension pot is used to provide a retirement income that rises each year with price inflation. If your employer will contribute too, the amount you need to save will be less than the sums shown in the table.

- you start to save sooner rather than later
- you delay the start of your retirement.

Rebekah's story

Rebekah is aged 38 and plans to retire at her state pension age of 68. She currently earns £36,000 a year and wants a retirement income of half this, £18,000 a year.

She expects to receive about £8,300 a year from her state pension and around £4,700 a year from workplace pensions. This puts her on track for an income of £13,000 a year in retirement. She needs a further £5,000 a year (£18,000 - £13,000) to reach her target.

She has 30 years until she retires, so she finds 30 along the bottom of the table, then works upwards to the row for age 68 (the planned start of her retirement). The figure there is £50. So, if she starts saving extra today, she needs to save £50 a month for each £1,000 of retirement income. Since she needs £5,000 of extra income, she should start saving an extra £250 a month (£5,000 ÷ £1,000 × £50) on top of what she is saving already.

If she delays starting to save extra for five years (when she will be age 43), she realises she will have to save even more. She would then have only 25 years left to save. Finding '25' on the bottom of the table and working up to the row for '68', Rebekah sees she would have to start saving £63 a month for each extra £1,000 of income, a total of £315 a month.

Arif's story

Arif plans to retire at 65. Aged 55 now, he has just ten more years to go, but he's £1,000 a year short of his retirement income goal. He finds '10' along the bottom of the table and works up to the row for age '65'. This tells him he needs to start saving an extra £195 a month to provide the extra £1,000 of pension. If he can put off retiring until age 70, he'll have 15 years left to save and his pension will not have to be paid out for so long. He finds '15' along the bottom of the table and works up to the row for '70' to find that, in this case, he would need to save only £105 a month to generate the extra £1,000 a year retirement income.

Ways to save extra

Your employer might have set up an arrangement that helps you save extra for retirement – often called an **additional voluntary contribution** (AVC) scheme. Some employers will match your extra savings up to a limit. For example, if you pay in an extra £10 a month, your employer might double that to £20.

Alternatively, you can make your own extra savings for retirement. The government still helps towards the cost of saving if you choose a personal pension scheme (as described on p. 147) or an individual savings account (ISA) (see Chapter 3).

Action point: Your pension scheme's website or booklet or your human resources department can tell you whether there are additional voluntary contribution (AVC) arrangements in your workplace.

Different pensions you might have

Your state pension

You can get your state pension once you reach state pension age. You cannot start it earlier. You can choose to start your state pension later, in which case the amount you get is increased.

While not especially generous, the state pension is likely to be the cornerstone of your retirement income. At the time of writing (2017–18), the standard amount was just under £8,300 a year (a little over £690 a month).

Since April 2016, men and women each build up their own state pension and you do this by paying National Insurance contributions while you are working. In some situations you may be credited with National Insurance and these credits count towards your state pension too – for example, if you're unemployed, ill, disabled or caring for a young child or elderly person, or your earnings are very low.

You might qualify for more or less than the standard amount of state pension, depending on your particular circumstances.

Action point: Check how much state pension you might from what age get by asking for a **state pension statement** or get a rough idea using the state pension calculator on the government website. Both are available by visiting GOV.uk*.

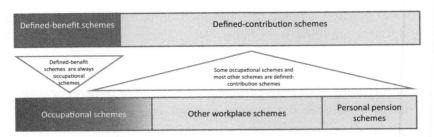

Figure 6.3 Types of pension scheme you might have

Source: Author's chart

Your workplace pension

To understand how much pension you might get and what your options are, you'll need to know what sort of pension scheme your workplace offers. The diagram shows the main types.

Pension schemes usually work in one of two ways:

- **Defined-benefit schemes**. These promise you a specified amount of pension usually linked to your pay. For example, in a **final salary scheme**, the pension equals a fraction of your pay just before retiring for every year you have been in the scheme. A **career average scheme** works in a similar way except that the pay is an average of your earnings during the whole period you've been in the scheme. See the case study, Julia, below. With this type of scheme, you have a pretty good idea of how much pension you'll end up with, making it easier to plan for retirement.
- **Defined-contribution schemes** (also called **money purchase schemes**). With these, you build up your own personal pot of savings. Money paid in is invested and hopefully grows. The pot of savings is then used to fund your retirement income. See the case study, Chang. It's hard to predict in advance how much retirement income you might get.

Some schemes are more complicated and combine elements of both defined-benefit and defined-contribution.

Pension schemes also differ according to who runs them. You might have:

- **Occupational pension** schemes (also called company schemes or superannuation). These are run by your employer. Defined-benefit schemes are always occupational schemes. But there are other occupational schemes that work on the defined-contribution basis. If you work in the public sector (for example, for local government, the emergency services, the National Health Service, Armed Forces or as teacher in a state school), you will usually be in an occupational scheme that works on the defined-benefit basis. In the private sector, some big firms still have defined-benefit occupational pension schemes.
- Other **workplace pension** schemes. Increasingly though, if you work in the private sector, you'll belong to a defined-contribution scheme and often it's a type of personal pension scheme.
- **Personal pension** schemes are run by insurance companies, 'platforms' (in other words, online investment services that let you choose and manage a wide range of funds and other investments) and other financial firms. Your employer chooses a scheme to be offered as the workplace scheme, but the arrangement is directly between you and the financial firm. You can also arrange your own personal pension scheme which has nothing to do with your workplace.

Action points: To find out what type of workplace pension scheme you belong to, visit your scheme's website, check any scheme booklet you received or contact your human resources department.

To arrange your own personal pension scheme, consider getting help from a financial adviser (see Chapter 8) or go direct to pension providers.

Julia's story

Julia belongs to a defined-benefit scheme. It promises her one-sixtieth of her average pay for each year she has been in the scheme. Because the value of money changes over time due to rising prices, pay for earlier years is increased in line with inflation before the average is worked out. She can get an idea of how much retirement income she might get using her current average pay, which is £30,000. By retirement, she will have been in the scheme 15 years. Using her scheme's pension formula, Julia's pension would be £30,000 × 1/60 × 15 = £7,500 or about a quarter of her pay.

Chang's story

Chang has been automatically enrolled into a defined-contribution scheme. He and his employer both pay in contributions and tax relief is added. The total paid in is 8% of Chang's pay. He's earning £30,000 at present, so £2,400 a year is going into his pension pot. It's impossible to know for sure how much retirement income it will provide but, on reasonable assumptions, his pension could be £1,700 a year when he retires in 15 years' time.

How safe is your defined-contribution pension?

If you are saving through a defined-contribution scheme, your savings are ring-fenced and should be secure. You're also protected by compensation schemes against loss due to dishonesty.

However, with a defined-contribution scheme, you are simply building up a pot of money not a particular level of pension. You bear the risks of your pension pot being too little to provide the pension you wanted because your investments did not grow as well as you'd hoped (investment risk), rising prices mean your pension buys less than you'd expected (**inflation risk**) or your money doesn't last as long as you do (**longevity risk**).

How safe is your defined-benefit pension?

If you are saving through a defined-benefit scheme, your employer promises you a set level of pension whatever happens. It's up to the employer to make sure there is enough money in the pension scheme to provide the promised pensions. Your employer – not you – bears the investment, inflation and longevity risks. The risk you will be worried about is: will your employer keep the promise?

Many employers have closed their defined-benefit pension schemes. You will still get the pensions you'd built up already up to the date of the closure. But you'll get less pension at retirement than you would have done had the scheme continued.

Defined-benefit schemes are regulated by The Pensions Regulator. These days many defined-benefit pension schemes do not have enough money to pay all the future pensions – in other words, the scheme has a deficit. The regulator makes employers set up a plan for reducing the deficit usually over a number of years. Sometimes, employers go bust and cannot pay off the deficit. In that case, you will still usually get most of your pension from a compensation scheme, called the Pension Protection Fund.

Action point: The people running an occupational scheme (whether defined-contribution or defined-benefit) will sort out any compensation due if things go wrong. With a personal pension scheme (whether arranged through the workplace or by yourself), you typically deal direct with the Financial Services Compensation Scheme*.

Thinking about pensions if you're over 50

Cashing in your defined-contribution savings

Pension schemes are intended mainly as a way of saving to provide an income in retirement. However, since April 2016, under new rules often called **freedom and choice**, you can take some or all of your savings out of your defined-contribution schemes whenever you like, provided you've reached a minimum age, currently 55. You can draw this money out in any combination of lump sums and/or income that you choose, but there may be tax to pay. Of course, any money you take out of your pension now reduces the income you'll have in retirement.

There are three different ways of drawing cash from your pension savings. They are illustrated in the diagram and explained below.

The basic principle is that, in total, you can get back a quarter of your savings tax-free, but the rest is taxable. There are three types of lump sum that you can draw out and this is how each is taxed:

1. Pre-retirement cash (technically called an **uncrystallised fund pension lump sum** or UFPLS): You're not ready to start a pension and just want cash. Provided the scheme allows it (occupational schemes usually don't), you can cash in part or all of your savings. A quarter of the amount you cash in is tax-free but the rest is added to your taxable income for the year and taxed in the normal way. You could lose a big chunk of your savings in tax.

2. Cash on retirement (technically called a **pension commencement lump sum** or PCLS): Although mainly intended for people who are ready to retire, you can also use this method if you are still in a pre-retirement stage of life. You can take up to a quarter of the total savings you have in the pension scheme as tax-free cash. This is a one-off option that you lose if you don't take it up. The rest of the savings are taxable when drawn out, but you don't actually have to start receiving any income just yet; you can just leave your savings sitting there until you are ready to start drawing a pension.

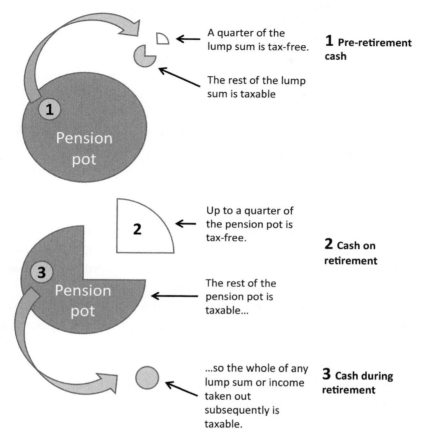

Figure 6.4 Different ways of taking cash out of your pension
Source: Author's chart

3. Cash during retirement: Once you've taken cash on retirement as above, you've had all the tax-free cash you're allowed. This means that any money you draw out now is added to your taxable income for the year and so the whole amount is taxed in the normal way.

Cash from a defined-benefit scheme

When you are ready to start your pension, you can take up to a quarter of the value of your pension rights as a tax-free lump sum (a pension commencement lump sum or PCLS). In some schemes, this is automatically paid; in others, you choose whether to give up part of your pension in exchange for this tax-free cash.

Income from a pension scheme

Whatever remains after you've had all your tax-free cash (see above) is intended to support you during retirement.

A defined-benefit scheme is very simple – it promises you a set level of pension. Once you reach the scheme's pension age, you can start to draw that income.

With a defined-contribution scheme, life is more complicated. You reach retirement with a pot of money and have to choose how to use that pot to finance the retirement you want. There are two basic options which are compared in the table.

Annuities and **drawdown** are both something of a gamble. With an **annuity**, you'll get a good deal if you live a long time and a poor deal if you die soon after retirement. You could view this as gambling with your pension pot. With drawdown, you don't know how long you'll live and so how long your money will have to last – so you're taking a gamble with your retirement income. My own research (Lowe,

Table 6.2 Main ways to take a retirement income

Insert Image A	Insert Image B
Lifetime annuity	**Drawdown**
Give up pension pot…	Keep pension pot
…in return get an income	Draw out income and/or lump sums when you choose
Income is secure, regular amount	Income may have to go down as well as up
Income is payable for life	Money might run out during retirement…
Income usually stops when you die	…or some might be left to pass on to your heirs

Source: Author's table

2017) shows that we tend to underestimate how long we will live. Figure 6.5 shows the average **life expectancy** for people of different ages now and also the surprisingly high chance of living to be a centenarian!

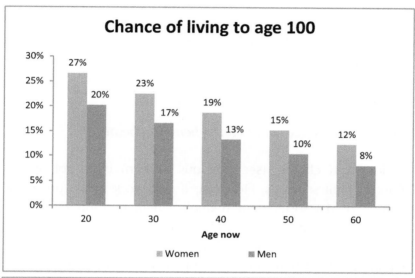

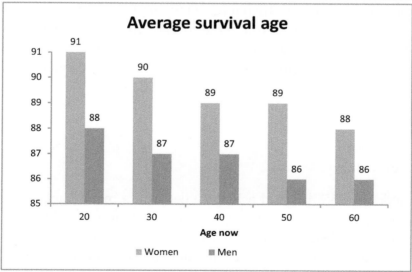

Figure 6.5 Age you might live to

Source: Author's chart, using data from ONS (2018)

However, annuities and drawdown don't have to be an 'either/or' option. You could split your pension pot, using part to ensure you have the minimum secure income you need and putting the rest into drawdown. You also have the option of using your remaining drawdown fund later on to buy an annuity.

> **Action point**: Make sure to shop around for an annuity or drawdown provider. The Money Advice Service* website has tools to help you.

'Freedom and choice' and defined-benefit schemes

'Freedom and choice' (see previous section) does not apply to defined-benefit schemes. However, if you work in the private sector, you could transfer your defined-benefit pension rights into a defined-contribution scheme and so access freedom and choice that way. You don't have this option if you're in a public sector scheme.

Defined-benefit pensions are valuable for you but expensive for employers to provide. Therefore, some employers offer mouth-watering transfer terms if you agree to give up your defined-benefit pension – see the case study of Jed. But do think hard before doing this – you'll be losing the secure pension that a defined-benefit scheme promises.

Jed's story

Jed, aged 55, has had a long career with a major bank. He's due to get a pension of £30,000 a year from its defined-benefit pension scheme when he reaches age 65. Once it starts, this pension will be increased each year in line with inflation and, if Jed dies first, a pension equal to half the amount he was getting will carry on being paid to his partner.

Recently, the bank has offered Jed £900,000 if he will give up his pension. The £900,000 must be transferred to another pension scheme. Jed is tempted and is planning to put the transfer value into a personal pension and immediately start drawdown. This means he can take a quarter of the £900,000 as a tax-free lump sum – this comes to £225,000 which he will use to pay off his mortgage. He will not draw any retirement income just yet, so the remaining £675,000 will stay invested in his drawdown fund until he needs it.

If Jed had to buy an annuity to provide a secure index-linked pension of £30,000 from age 65 with a 50% survivor pension, in late 2017 this could cost him over £1 million. Arguably then, the bank's offer of £900,000 falls short of the full value of his bank pension. Using drawdown, Jed cannot be sure how much retirement income he'll get – it all depends on how investments perform and how long Jed lives.

Getting advice

Your employer may arrange sessions at work where you can get information and advice about the workplace pension scheme and any arrangement for saving extra.

If you are planning to transfer money out of a defined-benefit pension scheme (or some other schemes that provide secure pensions – for example by guaranteeing a minimum amount of income from an annuity), you may be required by law to first get advice from a professional financial adviser.

Otherwise, you can at any time yourself choose and contact a professional financial adviser to give you advice about your pensions. In the case of a defined-contribution scheme, you may be able to use part of your pension pot to pay up to £500 towards that advice if your pension scheme offers this arrangement.

Action point: To find a professional financial adviser*, use a search service such as Unbiased* www.unbiased.co.uk or one of the other services listed in Chapter 8. To find out about using your pension pot to pay for advice, contact the pension provider concerned.

Conclusion

Whatever your age, you should be planning ahead for the time when you no longer want to work. The good news is that your employer usually helps towards the cost of saving for a pension.

That help is usually especially valuable if you belong to a defined-benefit scheme (in other words, a scheme that promises you a specified amount of pension). Therefore, do think carefully before giving up that type of pension.

Outside the public sector, it's more common these days to belong to a defined-contribution scheme where you build up your own personal pot of savings. Since April 2016, you've been able to draw cash out of these schemes from age 55 onwards. Bear in mind that drawing out cash early will reduce your retirement income later on.

References

Centre for Research in Social Policy (2018) *Minimum Income Calculator* [online] www.minimumincome.org.uk (accessed 15 June 2018).

Department for Work and Pensions (DWP) (2017) *State Pension Age Review* [online] www.gov.uk/government/uploads/system/uploads/attachment_data/file/630065/state-pension-age-review-final-report.pdf (accessed 15 June 2017).

HMSO (2014) *Pensions Act 2014: Elizabeth II. Chapter 19* [online] www.legislation.gov.uk/ukpga/2014/19/contents (accessed 15 June 2018).

HMSO (2011). *Pensions Act 2011: Elizabeth II. Chapter 19* [online] www.legislation.gov.uk/ukpga/2011/19/contents (accessed 15 June 2018).

HMSO (2007) *Pensions Act 2007: Elizabeth II. Chapter 22* [online] www.legislation.gov.uk/ukpga/2007/22/contents (accessed 15 June 2018).

Kahneman, D. (2011) *Thinking, Fast and Slow* London, Penguin.

Lowe, J. (2017) 'Longevity perceptions. An issue for pension guidance'. Working paper [online] www.open.ac.uk/business-school-research/pufin/sites/www.open.ac.uk.business-school-research.pufin/files/files/Longevity-perceptions_Jonquil-Lowe.pdf (accessed 15 June 2018).

Money Advice Service (MAS) (2018) *Compare Guaranteed Income Products* [online] https://comparison.moneyadviceservice.org.uk/en/tools/annuities (accessed 3 November 2017).

NEST (2014) 'Price of a comfortable retirement is £15k a year, new research finds'. Press release 19 May [online] www.nestpensions.org.uk/schemeweb/NestWeb/includes/public/news/price-of-a-comfortable-retirement.html (accessed 15 June 2018).

Office for National Statistics (2018) *How long will my pension need to last?* [online] https://visual.ons.gov.uk/how-long-will-my-pension-need-to-last/ (accessed 7 February 2018).

The Pensions Regulator (TPR) (nda) *Minimum Contribution Increases Planned by Law (Phasing)* [online] www.thepensionsregulator.gov.uk/phasing-minimum-contribution-increases-automatic-enrolment-advisers.aspx (accessed 15 June 2018).

The Pensions Regulator (TPR) (ndb) *Automatic Enrolment Earnings Thresholds* [online] www.thepensionsregulator.gov.uk/automatic-enrolment-earnings-threshold.aspx (accessed 15 June 2018).

Managing loans and credit

Jonquil Lowe

In a nutshell:

- **Debt can be useful in the right situation.**
- **Your employer may be a source of cheap or free loans.**
- **Help is available if debts become a problem.**

Borrowing is an everyday part of life. Another name for loans and credit is 'debt' but for most of us 'debt' sounds like something bad – more so in some languages, for example German where the word for debt 'Schuld' also means 'guilt'. But debt can open up opportunities and smooth out cash flow. It only becomes bad if you stop being in charge and debt starts to control you.

This chapter is about how to manage debt effectively, the loans that may be available from your employer or through your workplace and how to get back on track if your debts have become a problem.

Good and bad debt

Some years ago, money-saving expert, Martin Lewis (OUBS, 2013), gave a talk where I work and got us playing, pantomime style, the 'good-debt-bad-debt game'. Here's the gist of what he asked – how would you have answered?

1. I've been saving to buy a home, have a good deposit and the fixed-rate mortgage repayments are cheaper than the rent I've been paying. Good debt? Bad debt?
2. I've decided to go on an amazing holiday. It'll cost me some thousands but I'll put it on my credit card and sort out how to pay it off later. Good debt? Bad debt?
3. I need a car to get me to work and I'm taking out a loan to buy it. Good debt? Bad debt?
4. I'm unemployed and need a car to get to a job interview. It's 50–50 I'll get the job. I'll take out a loan to buy the car. Good debt? Bad debt?

I like this game because it highlights that borrowing is not just black and white. In the diagram below, I've drawn a scale from good to bad and suggested where some different debts might lie.

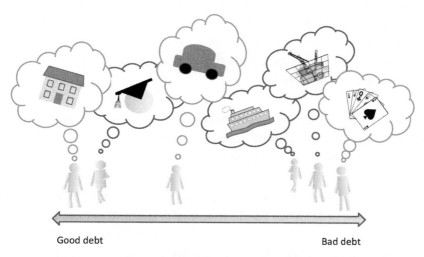

Good debt   Bad debt

Figure 7.1 Good and bad debt depends partly on why you are borrowing

Source: Author's chart

There are lots more debts you could add to the diagram and, of the ones I've included, you might put them in a different place to me, but here's my reasoning.

Good debts are either an investment aimed at improving your future or they pay for themselves because they displace other spending:

- Debt for investment: for example, getting qualifications or training with the aim of boosting your future earnings or increasing your happiness through being able to switch to a job that you like better than the one you have now. It also includes borrowing to start a business.
- Debts that pay for themselves: for example, buying a home – not because you think it will increase in value and make you a profit (though it might) – but because most of us have to pay out for somewhere to live. If buying with a mortgage saves you roughly the same in rent, then the borrowing pays for itself.
- Grey areas: then there are debts like the car loans Martin Lewis asked about. If you need a car to get to work, that could be classed as an investment that is helping you to boost your income and it may also pay for itself if it displaces fares for public transport. But borrowing to buy a car to get you to interviews might not be such a great idea if there's a high risk of not getting the job – better to get a lift or take a bus.

Bad debts include borrowing when you don't have a clear plan for repayment, when spending regularly exceeds your income, or you expose yourself to a dangerous level of risk.

- No clear plan for repayment: Martin's example of buying an expensive holiday on credit is something many people do. Fine if you know you can pay off the debt quickly but a bad idea if that debt is going to be a drag on your finances for years to come.
- Spending exceeds income: if you're regularly getting into debt just to pay for essentials like the weekly shop, this is a strong signal that you have a debt problem. You need to take action and

might want to skip ahead to the section below: *Dealing with debt problems*. Borrowing to feed any sort of addictive behaviour, such as alcohol, drugs or gambling, is also often associated with debt problems. It's important to get help with the underlying problem as well as the debts. NHS Choices* has useful information and details of organisations that can help.

- Dangerous level of risk: definitely risky is borrowing to invest money in say shares that you hope will rise in value but which might just as easily fall. For more on that, see the section below called *Speculate to accumulate?*

Of course, good or bad, it's essential that you can afford to make the repayments. As well as paying back the original sum you borrow, on top you'll normally have to pay interest and sometimes other charges as well.

Borrowing to buy a home

Few people can buy a home for cash, so it's usual to take out a mortgage. A mortgage is a loan secured against your home. 'Secured' means the lender can seize your home and sell it to get its money back if you don't make the agreed payments. In other words, you could lose your home if you don't keep up the repayments.

There are two main types of mortgage as shown in Figure 7.2.

These days, you'll normally get a **repayment mortgage**. This starts out with a set level of repayments that, provided you pay them all, means the loan is paid off in full by the end of the mortgage term. You then own your home outright! If this is a variable-rate mortgage, your repayments will be adjusted whenever interest rates change. However, you might opt to pay a fixed rate of interest for at least an initial period and, in that case, whatever happens to other interest rates, your payments don't change – that makes it easier to budget each month.

The alternative is an **interest-only mortgage**. You just pay interest on the loan each month (which can be variable or fixed). The amount you originally borrowed stays the same and, at the end of the

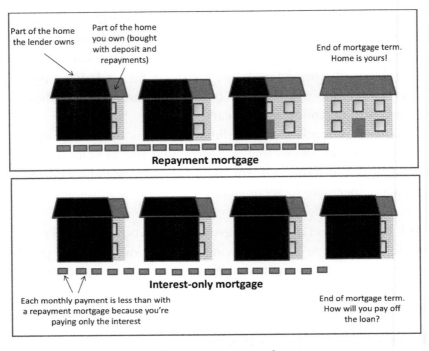

Figure 7.2 The two main types of mortgage

Source: Author's chart

mortgage term, you'll have to find a way to pay it back. If you don't, your home will be sold to pay off the mortgage and you'll have to find somewhere else to live. In the past, many people taking out this type of mortgage, also started a regular savings scheme called an **endowment policy** – hence these were called **endowment mortgages**. The aim was that the savings scheme would build up a sum large enough to pay off the mortgage at the end of the term. But there's no guarantee that the savings will grow by enough.

What to do if you have an interest-only mortgage

- If you have an endowment policy or other savings scheme, check regularly to see if it's on track to pay off the loan. If not consider the options below.

- If you don't have any plan for paying off your mortgage when it ends, talk to your lender urgently.
- Options for plugging the gap if you're not on track to pay off your mortgage:
  - o Switch to a repayment mortgage (possibly extending the term too).
  - o Increase your monthly payments.
  - o Pay off what you can with a lump sum, for example, from a pension scheme (see Chapter 6) or an inheritance.
  - o Extend your mortgage term to give yourself more time to plan.
- Talk to a mortgage adviser*.
- Don't do nothing!

Speculate to accumulate?

Borrowing to invest in a home or any other venture is a risky business, because borrowing magnifies gains but also losses.

Suppose I invest £100 of my money on the **stock market** and my shares go up by 10% to £110: I've made a profit of £10. Suppose instead I invest £100 of my money and borrow £900 (let's say from a friend who's happy not to charge me any interest) to boost my investment to £1,000. It goes up 10% to £1,100. I pay back the borrowed money and this time my profit is £100. So borrowing to invest has increased my profit tenfold. Not bad!

Now, see what happens if the investment falls by 10% instead of rising. If I invest £100 of my own money, I get back only £90, leaving me nursing a loss of £10. If instead I invest £100 of my own money plus £900 I've borrowed (total £1,000), a 10% fall means I get back only £900. I pay back the borrowed money but am left with nothing – I've lost all my money.

So what makes buying a home with a mortgage seem like such a fool-proof investment? Well, of course, it's not fool-proof because house prices can and do fall. But, given that the majority of voters are still homebuyers or own their home outright, government policies have tended to support house prices. There's no guarantee that this will be the case in future, so it is safer to borrow for a home as a place to live rather than as an investment.

Borrowing for other reasons

There are many different ways to borrow money. Some of the most common are shown in the chart below. It's hard to generalise when comparing the cost of different types of debt because what you'll pay depends partly on your particular circumstances. But the chart suggests a rough order of cost.

Below are a few details about each of these loans and some hybrid types of borrowing (**personal contract purchase** (PCP) for buying a car and student loans).

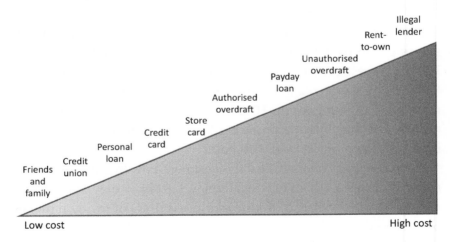

Figure 7.3 Typical cost of different types of borrowing compared

Source: Author's chart

Cheapest ways to borrow

You may be able to borrow from family and friends. For example, around one person in eight says they would turn to friends or family if faced with an unexpected urgent bill of £200 (Rowlingson and McKay, 2017). Family and friends are less likely to charge you interest and may be willing to be flexible about repayments. Even so, many people are wary of borrowing this way in case it sours relationships.

Credit unions are mutual self-help groups. They are like community banks. Members of each credit union have a common bond which might be, say, living in the same area, working in the same industry or working for the same employer. They can be a source of affordable loans, especially if you find it hard to get mainstream borrowing. There is more about credit unions in the section below on *Loans and credit at work*.

Mainstream borrowing

If you can, you'll pay least for commercial borrowing if you can use mainstream sources, such as personal loans (from your own bank, other banks or through shops where you buy goods) and credit cards. However, both your access to these sources, and the amount you personally will pay depend on how creditworthy you are deemed to be – see *Why you might pay more for credit* below.

Personal loans are a type of **reducing-balance loan** – like the repayment mortgages described above, except the term is usually shorter (say one to five years) and the interest rate is typically fixed for the whole term of the loan. This means you pay back a set amount every month. So you know exactly how much you need to budget for and provided you stick to all the repayments, the loan will automatically be paid off in full.

Credit cards are very flexible but if you flex them too much they are costly. You choose how much to borrow up to the credit limit you're given. You borrow by paying for things in shops or online, or (not recommended because of extra charges) by withdrawing cash from

Figure 7.4 How total cost can increase if credit card debt lingers

Note: Assumes you borrow £1,000
Source: Author's chart

machines or at bureaux de change. Subject to a minimum amount, you choose how much to pay back each month. If you pay off the full balance every month – and just over half of card users do (Arrow Global cited in Jolly, 2016) – the credit is free. If you roll the debt over, you pay interest. There are extra charges if you miss a monthly payment or go over your credit limit. Credit cards can be convenient and relatively low cost if you borrow just for short periods, but become costly if you pay off only a little each month.

Store cards mostly work like credit cards, but the interest rate tends to be a higher – for example, in 2018, the average credit card rate was 18% (UK Finance, 2017) a year while store cards typically charged around 29% (Moneyfacts, 2018).

An **authorised overdraft** is where you agree with your bank that you can spend more than you have in your current account up to a limit and for a maximum period of time. Some accounts come with a small, free overdraft. For larger sums, you typically pay a monthly fee and an arrangement fee or interest.

Using cards wisely

- Get free credit by paying off your credit card(s) in full every month.
- Set up a direct debit to make sure you never miss a credit card repayment.
- Use a debit card rather than credit cards. With debit cards you directly spend the money in your bank account, so you are not running up debt (unless your bank account is overdrawn).
- Use credit cards for larger purchases. The law (HMSO, 1974, section 75) makes credit card providers jointly liable with the retailer when you used your card to buy something costing more than £100 and up to £30,000 and something goes wrong.

High-cost borrowing

Try to avoid the following forms of credit if you can because they are costly.

Payday loans are short-term (say, 30-day) loans aimed to tide you over until the next payday. The cost of payday loans used to be sky high with interest rates equivalent to 5,000% a year! However, since 2015, the amount you can be charged is capped at a maximum of 0.8% per day of the original sum borrowed (equal to 292% a year) and the total interest and charges are capped at 100% (FCA, 2014), so the most you should have to pay back is double the amount you borrowed.

In 2017, the cap on payday loans was reviewed, along with the market for other high-cost credit. The UK regulator said it was worried about other forms of high-cost credit, in particular:

- **Unauthorised overdrafts**. These are where you go overdrawn on your current account without asking your bank first. You quickly start to rack up hefty monthly fees, high interest rates and/or other charges. Consumer organisation, Which?, found that some high-street banks would charge 7 ½ times more than the payday loan cap for a 30-day £100 unauthorised overdraft (Which?, 2017).

- **Rent-to-own deals** which are the modern equivalent of **hire purchase** (HP), but higher cost. The principle of hire purchase is that you get to use the goods you want straight away, but don't own them outright until you've finished making regular payments to the HP provider. With rent-to-own, you get household appliances, like fridges and washing machines, and furniture from the retailer, paying gradually through typically weekly instalments. The ticket price of the goods is often inflated, the interest rate charged on the instalment plans high and you may be persuaded to take out expensive insurance to cover the goods. You could easily end up paying two or three times the normal price for these goods if you use rent-to-own. But some organisations, such as the Fair for You* website www.fairforyou.co.uk and local housing associations, have set up their own lower-cost alternative rent-to-own schemes.

In May 2018, the regulator announced plans to address some of the problems with these types of credit (FCA, 2018). The plans, which are subject to consultation, include a proposed cap on the cost of rent-to-own deals and greater transparency about the costs of overdrafts (though no cap on their cost).

To offer loans and credit, UK lenders must be regulated by the Financial Conduct Authority. This means the worst sales practices are banned and, if things go wrong, you have access to a complaints system including the free-to-use impartial Financial Ombudsman Service*. Avoid borrowing from an **illegal lender** (also known as loan sharks) – you will not get the safeguards and illegal lenders often use ugly tactics to get the repayments.

Action points:
- Check if a lender is regulated by searching the Financial Services Register*.
- Report illegal lenders (anonymously) to the illegal money lending team* for your part of the UK.

Borrowing to buy a car

There have long been many ways to buy a car – cash, hire purchase, personal loan arranged by the car dealership or that you source elsewhere. But the trendy way to buy a car these days is a personal contract plan (PCP).

With a PCP, you do not set out to buy the whole car. Instead, you effectively lease the car and, after a few years, you have several options. You can pay a lump sum (sometimes called a 'balloon payment') and the car becomes yours; you can get a different car with a new PCP deal; or you can just walk away (literally because you'll have no car).

In theory, the monthly payments for a PCP are cheaper than taking out a loan to cover the full price of a car. In practice, people often look at how much they can afford and then trade up to the snazziest car they can get.

There's nothing wrong with PCP, but you need to be aware that the car is not actually yours (unless you make the balloon payment), and there are usually restrictions with penalty payments for breaking them. For example, you'll agree to a maximum mileage limit and also have to pay for any damage the car suffers during the time you have it.

Student loans

If you've gone to university from the late 1990s onwards, you probably had or still have a student loan. This is different from other forms of borrowing (and some experts argue these loans are a graduate tax rather than borrowing).

- You make repayments only if your income exceeds a given threshold (which varies across the countries of the UK and depends on when you took out the loan) – for example, around £18,000 or £25,000 a year.
- Your repayments are 9% of your income above the threshold.

- Your employer must automatically collect the repayments from your pay.
- If your income is low or drops below the threshold – for example, because you become ill or unemployed – the repayments stop until your income recovers.
- Interest is charged on the loan even during periods when you're not making repayments.
- Any outstanding amount is written off after a set term – again this varies across the countries of the UK and when you took out the loan but is usually 25 or 30 years. It's also written off on death, but not bankruptcy.

Since the repayments stop if your earnings drop, student loans are less of a problem than other debt if you're going through a rough patch. On the other hand, the repayments reduce your ability to take on and manage other debt, such as a mortgage to buy a home.

Loans and credit at work

In addition to pay, jobs come with a range of non-pay add-ons, called **benefits in kind**, such as a pension scheme, and, in some cases, cheap or free loans and access to savings schemes.

Season ticket loan and other cheap loans

If you travel to work by public transport, an annual season ticket might cut the cost by around 15% (nearly one-sixth) compared with buying a weekly ticket. But shelling out for an annual ticket can be a tall order (see Rasheed's case study below), so some employers help out by providing a free season ticket loan.

If you work for a financial services firm (such as a bank or building society), you might be able to take out other loans through work too, either free or more likely at a preferential interest rate.

You pay income tax and National Insurance contributions on your normal pay (unless it's very low). Similarly, you may have to pay

Figure 7.5 A season ticket loan could cut your travel-to-work costs by nearly one-sixth

Source: Author's diagram

extra income tax if you get some benefits in kind from work, but not National Insurance. However, in the case of cheap or free loans, there is no extra tax to pay provided the total of the loans is less than a maximum limit, which in early 2018 was £10,000.

If the total of your loans is more than £10,000 throughout the whole tax year, then you pay tax on the difference between the interest rate you actually pay and an official rate published by the government. In early 2018, the official rate was 3% a year (HMRC, 2018). (A tax year runs from 6 April one year to 5 April the next. For example, the 2018–19 tax year is 6 April 2018 to 5 April 2019.) Your employer should tell you if tax is due and you may then need to complete a tax return – there is guidance on how to do this on the government website, GOV.uk*.

Rasheed's story

Rasheed lives in Winchester and commutes into the City of London each work day. A weekly season ticket, including tube travel, costs him £150.20 (an average of £30 per day). According to the National Rail (2018) season ticket calculator, in March 2018, a yearly season ticket would cost him £6,008 or just £25.57 per day, assuming that he has five weeks holiday per year – a saving of around 15% compared with weekly tickets. He takes up an interest-free season ticket loan from his employer to buy the annual ticket; repayments of just over £500 are automatically deducted from his pay packet each month. This is the only employer loan that Rasheed has, so there is no tax to pay on this benefit in kind.

Credit unions

You have already seen in Chapter 3 (p. 58) how a credit union at work can help you save easily. They can also be a source of relatively cheap loans.

Credit unions are not-for-profit organisations that help their members to save and borrow. Members must have a common bond and this can be that you all work for the same employer or in the same industry. The money paid in by employees who save provides the funds which are lent out to those who borrow.

The main advantage for savers is that it helps you to commit to good savings habits because normally you can arrange for a set amount of saving to be deducted regularly direct from your pay packet. However, the return you get is often lower than from a bank or building society.

Where credit unions come into their own is if you want to borrow. The process is usually quick and friendly and cheaper than, say, payday loans and rent-to-own. By law, the maximum interest rate that a credit union can charge is 3% a month (HMSO, 2013) – equivalent to 42.6% a year – but many charge less. The maximum rate is lower in Northern Ireland at 1% (12.68% a year).

Your workplace credit union might also provide other services or benefits. For example, some credit unions run bill-paying accounts or 'managed' current accounts that let you ensure that all your essential bills are met as soon as your pay comes in. And some offer life insurance, so that in the event of death your survivors get an additional lump sum on top of just the return of your savings.

Your HR department should be able to tell you if there is a credit union operating in your workplace. For more information about credit unions*, see *Useful contacts*.

Jasmine's story

Jasmine's washing machine gave up the ghost – no joke, as she has three young children. She looked at taking out a credit card to pay for a new machine, costing £200. The card would have an interest rate of 35% a year interest. If she'd paid off the debt over, say, 18 months, it would have cost just under £14 a month and the total she'd have paid back would be £252. However, the credit union at work was willing to lend her £200 for 18 months at a rate of 1% a month (12.68% a year). Her monthly repayments of £12.20 are deducted direct from her pay before she gets it, and the total she'll repay is just £220.

Salary loan schemes

Some employers are partnering with third-party firms which special-ise in providing and managing loans for employees. The key feature of these schemes is that a regular sum is deducted automatically from your salary before you get it to repay the loan. Salary loans can be particularly useful as a way of paying off more expensive debts, such as overdrafts, payday loans and credit card debt, and for coping with an unexpected expense if you don't have an emergency fund.

Personal loans taken out through a salary loan scheme are likely to be cheaper than a loan that you arrange for yourself, because the automated repayments through salary deduction scheme mean the lender can be confident of getting its money back. They also provide you with the discipline to tackle paying off debts that you might oth-erwise be tempted continually to put off until tomorrow – because of those pesky behavioural traits that we all have.

The third-party partner also often offers automated transfers from your salary into savings schemes. Similar to workplace credit unions, the combination of loans, savings and automated deductions from salary can help you take control of your money and develop good financial habits.

Ask your HR department at work if there is a salary loan scheme you can join.

Why you might pay more for credit

Commercial lenders use fairly standard information to try to assess the risk of lending you money. The risk from their point of view is that you won't keep up the agreed repayments. Perversely, the higher they deem that risk to be, the more they'll charge you, making it even harder to afford the repayments!

If you look too high a risk, mainstream lenders will turn you down altogether, which is why so many people end up with high-cost forms of credit.

What makes you a good or bad credit risk?

Lenders base their judgement about you as a credit risk on information they collect on the application form and from specialist firms called **credit reference agencies** (CRAs). There are three main CRAs operating in the UK: Experian*, Equifax* and TransUnion* (formerly called CallCredit). They each hold a file on virtually every adult in the UK that includes:

- Your identity and address based on the electoral register.
- Your history of managing borrowing and bills from the firms who supply you with credit. This includes services where you pay in arrears, such as quarterly energy bills.
- Public information, such as court judgements and bankruptcy orders about any debts you've defaulted on. These still stay on your credit file for six years after the judgement or order has expired.

It's not just bad experiences on your credit file that can make you look a poor credit risk. Lack of data – called a 'thin' credit history will do that too. Some newer, smaller CRAs (such as CredScope* www.credscope.com) aim to address that by allowing you to supply relevant information that's either non-standard or not in the format that the big CRAs use.

You have the right to get the information held about you by each CRA on payment of a statutory fee of £2 and to have any incorrect

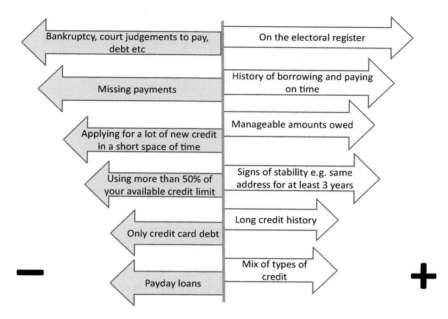

Figure 7.6 Factors that tend to make you a worse or better credit risk

Source: Author's chart

information put right. Be aware that, with services that give you access to your file for 'free', you are usually paying with your personal data which can be sold on to other organisations or used to target you with advertisements.

Your credit score

Most lenders take all this information about you and use it to calculate your **credit score**. If your score is below a threshold set by the lender, it will turn you down. If you're accepted, the higher your score, the lower the interest rate you are likely to be charged.

It's a common fallacy that you have one credit score. Not so! Every lender calculates its own credit score for you. However, you can get an indicative credit score from the CRAs and other organisations. It is based on the information held about you by a CRA and will give you an idea of how creditworthy you are likely to seem if you do apply for a loan or other credit.

Secured and unsecured loans

A **secured loan** is one where the borrower can seize something you own as a way of getting its money back if you don't keep up the payments.

The most common type of secured loan is a mortgage, in other words a loan secured against your home. Mortgages are not just for buying a home. They also come in the form of top-up loans – for example, to pay for home improvements. They are also used as consolidation loans. This is where you take out a single loan secured against your home to replace other more costly loans.

Other secured loans are log-book loans, which are secured against your car, pawnbroker loans secured against the item you pawn, and hire purchase where you don't own the item until all the payments have been made.

Secured loans should be easier to get and cheaper than an equivalent **unsecured loan**, because the borrower is bearing less risk. By the same token, you are bearing more risk: if you don't keep up the payments, you're likely to lose your home, car or other item against which the loan is secured.

Dealing with debt problems

If you go overdrawn most months, rely on payday loans or other high-cost credit, never make a dent in your credit card balance or stuff bills and reminders out of sight, you have a debt problem.

Debt problems get worse if you ignore them, so the time to sort them out is: NOW.

There's nothing unusual or awful about having a debt problem. It's estimated that over 8 million (Webb, 2017) people in the UK have a debt problem – that's one person in six! If that includes you, you are definitely not alone.

Debt problems build up or come out of the blue for all sorts of reasons – we are all bombarded with marketing encouraging us to borrow and spend, debt that's affordable one moment can become out of control if circumstances change because of, say, job loss, illness, relationship breakdown or a rise in interest rates. There is no shame or stigma to being in debt. You just need to focus on sorting it out.

Six steps for sorting out a debt problem

The key steps for sorting out a debt problem are:

1. Be brave: acknowledge the problem exists.
2. Make a list of all your debts: to whom; amount owed in each case.
3. Make a record of all the money you currently have coming in and everything you spend. Now see what changes you can make to free up money to sort out your debts. This includes making sure that you are getting all the income you're entitled to, including any state benefits, as well as ways of cutting back on your spending.
4. Split your debts into priority and non-priority debts. Priority debts are the ones where the consequences of not paying them are severe – for example, losing your home, being sent to prison, having essential services cut off or losing vital assets such as a car you need to get to work. The diagram below shows the main priority debts.
5. Negotiate with the firms to which you owe the priority debts to pay them off at a rate you can afford. Ask them to stop charging interest while you do this.
6. Then negotiate with the other firms to which you owe non-priority debts.

You don't have to do this on your own. There are free, impartial debt advice agencies* throughout the UK who can give you guidance and help with all these steps. See Chapter 8 for details.

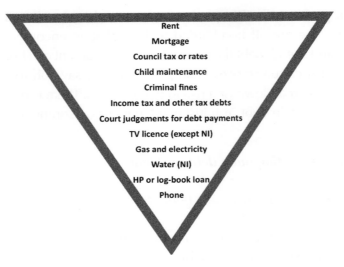

Figure 7.7 Priority debts: make sure you deal with these first
Note: NI = Northern Ireland.
Source: Author's chart

Conclusion

Debt is not always bad. There is a place for debt in anyone's life if it opens up opportunities or improves your future, and you can afford the repayments. But, if you can save up for something first, that will always be cheaper than borrowing to buy it.

There are various ways to keep down the cost of debt: make use of free or cheap loans from work; pay debt off as quickly as you can; look after your credit score; and don't overlook less usual lenders such as credit unions – check whether there is one at work. Secured loans are typically cheaper than unsecured, but bear in mind that they are risky for you because you could lose your home or other asset if you don't keep up the repayments.

It's easy for debts to get out of hand. Know the signs and take action quickly. Get help from the advice agencies discussed in Chapter 8.

References

Financial Conduct Authority (FCA) (2018) *Consultations on High Cost Credit and Overdrafts* [online] www.fca.org.uk/publications/consultation-papers/cp18-12-and-cp18-13-consultations-high-cost-credit-and-overdrafts (accessed 17 June 2018).

Financial Conduct Authority (FCA) (2014) *FCA Confirms Price Cap Rules for Payday Lenders*, Press release, 11 November [online] www.fca.org.uk/news/press-releases/fca-confirms-price-cap-rules-payday-lenders (accessed 17 June 2018).

HMSO (1974) *Consumer Credit Act 1974 Elizabeth II Chapter 39* ([online] www.legislation.gov.uk/ukpga/1974/39/section/75 (accessed 17 June 2018).

HMSO (2013) *The Credit Unions (Maximum Interest Rate on Loans) Order 2013* No 2589 [online] www.legislation.gov.uk/uksi/2013/2589/contents/made (accessed 17 June 2018).

HM Revenue & Customs (HMRC) (2018) *Beneficial Loan Arrangements – HMRC Official Rates* www.gov.uk/government/publications/rates-and-allowances-beneficial-loan-arrangements-hmrc-official-rates/beneficial-loan-arrangements-hmrc-official-rates (accessed 17 June 2018).

Jolly, J. (2016) *British Households Taking on More Debt as Almost Half Struggle to Pay Credit Card Bills On Time* [online] www.cityam.com/254918/british-households-taking-more-debt-almost-half-struggle (accessed 17 June 2018).

Moneyfacts (2018) Moneyfacts, 351(January).

National Rail (2018) *Season Ticket Calculator* [online] http://vt.nationalrail.co.uk/service/seasonticket/search (accessed 17 June 2018).

Open University Business School (OUBS) (2013) *Martin Lewis – PUFin* [online] www.youtube.com/embed/TDZq2ABAEfk (accessed 17 June 2018).

Rowlingson, K. and McKay, S. (2017) *Financial Inclusion Annual Monitoring Report 2017* [online] www.birmingham.ac.uk/Documents/news/15518-CHASM-Report-Stage-4.pdf (accessed 17 June 2018).

UK Finance (2017) *Quarterly Market Trends Q3 2017* [online] www.ukfinance.o3rg.uk/wp-content/uploads/2017/11/Quarterly-Market-Trends-Q3-2017.pdf (accessed 17 June 2018).

Webb, A. (2017) *Are You One of the 8.3 Million Adults With Problem Debt?* Money Advice Service blog [online] www.moneyadviceservice.org.uk/

blog/are-you-one-of-the-8-3-million-adults-with-problem-debt (accessed 17 June 2018).

Which? (2017) *Overdraft Charges Could Cost £156 More Than Payday Loans*. Press release, 8 February [online] https://press.which.co.uk/whichpressreleases/overdraft-charges-could-cost-156-more-than-payday-loans/ (accessed 17 June 2018).

Getting help and advice

Jason Butler

In a nutshell:

- Sometimes you might need to seek help with your personal finances, but that doesn't mean you can abdicate responsibility for decision making or your financial well-being.
- There are lots of sources of free information, support and guidance available to help you be better with money.
- Help and advice ranges from generic information through to highly regulated and personalised advice from a professional adviser.

When to get help and advice

Even if you are great at maths, there is still a high chance that you might not feel as confident as you would like to be at managing your money. That's entirely understandable and normal for a large proportion of the population.

As we discussed in Chapter 1, money can be a highly emotive issue and we don't always make rational decisions which are in our best interests. And in Chapter 2 we saw that very often day-to-day decisions are not always taken in the context of our wider and longer-term needs.

Getting help with your finances might be as simple as reading information on the subject (like this book), speaking to your employer's human resources department about your benefit package, getting help dealing with problem debt, or consulting a professional financial adviser about your entire financial situation.

Seeking knowledge and understanding of personal finance issues and how they relate to you is a good habit to develop. The more you know yourself and how to plan your money, the more likely you'll have better outcomes.

Figure 8.1 shows the different ways of problem solving. These range from highly directive, where someone solves your financial problems for you, through to non-directive, where you are helped to solve your own financial problems.

Why you might seek help or advice

There are times when seeking more personalised help is likely to be a good idea. Canadian neuropsychologist and executive coach Dr

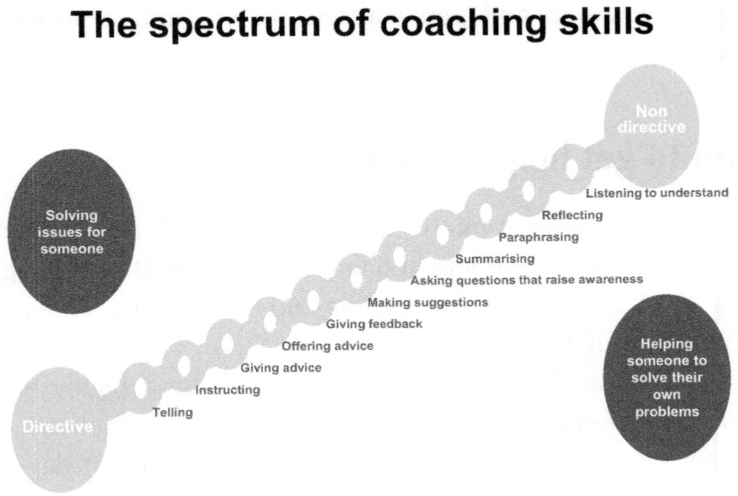

The spectrum of coaching skills

Non directive

Listening to understand
Reflecting
Paraphrasing
Summarising
Asking questions that raise awareness
Making suggestions
Giving feedback
Offering advice
Giving advice
Instructing
Telling

Solving issues for someone

Helping someone to solve their own problems

Directive

Figure 8.1 Ways to solve problems

Source: This material was developed by Simonne Gnessen of Wise Monkey Financial Coaching. Used by permission of Simonne Gnessen © 2017, originally adapted from Downey 2003.

Moira Somers (2018) suggests there are several reasons why people seek personalised advice:

1. To reduce complexity: it's easy to become overwhelmed and out of your depth if you have lots of unfamiliar terms, options and facts to assimilate. Experts can help you to cut through the information 'noise' and understand what's relevant to you.

2. To take action: many people suffer 'decisional paralysis', particularly when they have too many options or choices. An expert can help you avoid indecision and dithering and take appropriate action.

3. To save time: delegating certain financial related tasks can allow you to do things that are a better use of your time and energy.

4. To offload unpleasantness: although closely related to saving time, there can be immense value in getting someone else to do financial tasks you dislike doing, for example record keeping, thereby reducing stress and drudgery.

5. To make someone else happy: there are occasions, such as a major life transition or event, where seeking help and advice will be of indirect benefit to other people you know. Or someone else may have suggested you seek advice because they want you to be happier and make good financial decisions.

6. To increase confidence: consulting with a professional can give reassurance that you are on track to meet important financial goals and have made good decisions. An expert can also help you keep in check any over-confidence that might cause you to make a rushed or poor financial decision.

7. To help make better trade-offs: many questions can't be answered purely based on facts or financial analysis, but require an understanding of lifestyle issues, personal values and other factors. An experienced adviser can help you to reconcile the inevitable disconnects and dichotomies between what you want and what you can afford.

8. To receive encouragement: changing long-standing money habits and behaviours can be hard to sustain, particularly if they are

based on deep seated beliefs and ideas. Having the support and encouragement of someone who is on your side, and to whom you can be accountable, can keep you on track if you find yourself wavering.

9. To have someone to blame: recent research suggests that some people 'delegate primarily to cede responsibility and blame' rather than purely to obtain good advice. In the case of a couple, for example, this might reduce the risk of either party blaming each other if things don't go according to plan (Steffel et al., 2016).

10. To feel safer: when we have to make difficult financial decisions, studies show that the way our brains process information changes (by experiencing less activity) if we have the benefit of help and advice from a financial expert. In this situation, our brains look a lot more like when people feel a high level of trust and safety (Engelmann et al., 2009).

When to seek help or advice

- Redundancy (your employer will probably arrange professional support)
- A change of job that leads to a major change in your financial situation
- Serious debt problems
- Receipt of a significant inheritance
- Reviewing deferred guaranteed pension benefits
- Thinking about buying or deciding to buy a house
- Funding long-term care for a relative or yourself
- Being awarded a compensation payment or winning a cash prize (e.g. **Premium Bonds**)
- Suffering serious illness or disability that stops you or your partner from working
- The birth of a child or grandchild
- Death of your life partner or an elderly close relative

- Deciding how best to provide a lifetime income from accumulated financial assets, either at or leading up to the time when you stop or reduce paid work
- Sale of a business or property that changes your financial position in terms of income or capital.

Types of help and advice

There are various forms of financial help and advice as shown in summary in Figure 8.2.

Financial education

The starting point is **generic information** that you need to make sense of and then adapt to your personal needs. Educating yourself on basic money management principles and practices, as well as

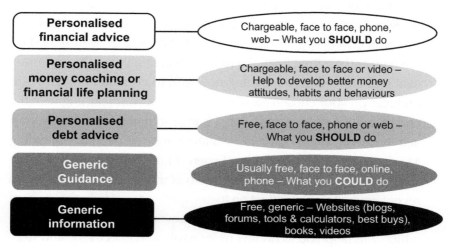

Personalised financial advice	Chargeable, face to face, phone, web – What you **SHOULD** do
Personalised money coaching or financial life planning	Chargeable, face to face or video – Help to develop better money attitudes, habits and behaviours
Personalised debt advice	Free, face to face, phone or web – What you **SHOULD** do
Generic Guidance	Usually free, face to face, online, phone – What you **COULD** do
Generic information	Free, generic – Websites (blogs, forums, tools & calculators, best buys), books, videos

Figure 8.2 The different types of financial help and advice

Source: Author's diagram

understanding what is and is not relevant to you, should help you work out whether you need more personalised help or advice.

For example, The Open University* offers three free online money management courses – for which website URLs can be found in the reference section at the end of this chapter:

- *Managing My Money** course: this course helps you to gain the skills to manage your personal finances: managing budgets, debts, investments, property purchase, pensions and insurance. You'll start by learning how to compile a budget and use it to make good decisions about your spending. You'll explore debts and investments and find out how mortgages are used to finance home ownership. The critical issue of pension planning is explained, with guidance on different pension products. You'll finish by examining different types of insurance and getting practical advice on how to make rational decisions about which insurance products to buy. Using up-to-the minute data from the UK you develop financial skills and approaches that are relevant globally. The course is rich in high-quality text, images, video, audio and interactive elements to support your learning.
- *Managing My Money for Young Adults** course: this course is designed for young people who have recently left school or are still studying, about to start on an apprenticeship or thinking about university. It covers everything you need to know to get you started on the new and exciting financial journey that lies ahead. It offers practical tips on what to start doing now and to continue doing as you progress on your chosen path. You can check your learning with the end-of-session quizzes and gain a badge so that you can share your achievement. Video interviews feature money experts, including Martin Lewis of Money Saving Expert. Plus, there are real-life case studies featuring current students (both at school and university) and recent graduates who reflect on their experiences of living away from home for the first time while studying. It even features a bespoke app which will help you to budget more easily and effectively, and step-by-step animations to guide you through tricky financial processes.

- *Managing My Investments** course: on this free online course, you'll learn about different investment choices, the returns and risks associated with each, and the evidence about their historical performance. You'll explore investment strategies, as well as the practicalities about involvement in personal finance markets. And you'll look at how to avoid the individual and group behavioural traits that can impair effective investment decision making.

Guidance

The next level of help is guidance on the particular issue(s) that relates to you. This sets out what you MIGHT do, but is NOT PERSONALISED ADVICE. Guidance can be on general financial issues, with no product related solution, or focused on particular products or services, such as investing or pensions.

Companies like Nutmeg*, Scaleable Capital*, Moola*, and Wealthify* all offer investment **guidance** for long-term investing, but they don't help with wider financial planning needs.

Some employers provide guidance from **financial advice** firms, with the option to extend this to **personalised financial advice**. Check with your employer what is available, as this is likely to be more comprehensive than any of the online investment focused companies.

Money coaching/therapy

Money coaching/therapy is a relatively new field that combines psychology, financial education and support, to help people make better financial decisions.

The coach/therapist helps people to understand their relationship with money, working through any issues or obstacles. They then help the person to understand and navigate their financial options, such that they improve their confidence and capability in relation to money; the overall aim is to empower the individual to take control of and responsibility for their financial well-being.

Figure 8.3 Role of a financial coach or therapist

Source: This material was developed by Simonne Gnessen of Wise Monkey Financial Coaching. Used by permission of Simonne Gnessen © 2017

Financial coaches/therapists typically charge £50–125 per hour, with the typical engagement lasting between 3–10 hours. Compared to the cost of regulated comprehensive financial advice/planning, coaching/therapy is both much more affordable and usually delivers quicker results in the form of improved emotions, feelings and money capabilities.

The majority of financial coaches or therapists do not provide **regulated financial advice** and related services, but they usually have links with firms that do, should such advice be required.

Financial life planning

Financial life planning is a consultative approach based on the premise that each person needs to discover their essential goals in life before they go on to formulate a financial plan, so that their personal finances support those important goals.

The Kinder Institute, founded by George Kinder, is the leading organ-isation that trains financial advisers in financial life planning skills. Kinder Institute (2018) describes financial life planning as follows:

> What's really important is your LIFE, not your money. This may sound elementary but few of us spontaneously undertake a thoughtful inquiry into our deepest and most enduring values and objectives. Tradition-ally financial advisors have focused on the numbers – budgeting, in-vestments, taxes, or insurance – without exploring the broader context. They rarely ask questions like:
>
> 'If you had more time or money, what would you do?'
>
> 'What do you want to accomplish or attain so you will feel that you've had a life well-lived?'
>
> 'What moves, touches, or inspires you?'
>
> Our advisors are trained to ask such questions and, just as important, listen to your answers. They therefore become your partner in clarify-ing and achieving your most meaningful and deeply felt aspirations. We call it Life Planning because what's really important isn't your mon-ey, it's your life.

Most, but not all, financial life planners also provide personalised regulated financial advice and related products and services, to help your lifestyle vision become a reality. However, there is no reason why you couldn't engage a financial life planner to help you define your lifestyle vision and how money fits into that, and then arrange finan-cial products yourself or with another (possibly lower cost) provider.

Personal advice

Personal advice is tailored to your specific situation and is either:

- free, personalised advice on problem debt or
- paid for personalised advice on either a specific issue or your overall financial situation.

While there are lots of debt management companies around who will help you deal with problem debt for a fee, **there is absolutely**

no need to pay for this advice. Citizens Advice Bureau* and several other charities provide free debt counselling to individuals.

Lorraine's story

Lorraine, Dave and their three teenaged children lived with Lorraine's parents. Lorraine was the primary carer for her mum, who was seriously ill. Her mum eventually died and shortly afterwards Lorraine had a big argument with her dad which meant she and her family had to move out, into temporary accommodation.

'I got some help with setting up our new home but still had things I had to buy', says Lorraine. 'Nothing fancy, just basics to make it comfortable for my kids. My only option was to use credit cards and catalogues.

'Our place was in Woolwich and it was too far to expect them to walk each day [to Eltham]. But as the journey was less than three miles I wasn't able to get help with the fares. Things just escalated from there. Then we were moved to Eltham. It was great to be near the kids' schools but it meant setting up a new home all over again.

'Soon I was taking out loans to try and consolidate the debts, but the payments kept growing and I was left with no money to live off. It got totally out of control. I went to a debt management company and ended up paying £500 a month, with a huge chunk of that going on admin fees.

'Some of the debts were going down, but very slowly. And I was left with nothing to get by on.' Things got even worse when Dave had to give up his job as a mechanic due to ill health, causing him and Lorraine to live apart so they could get the maximum state benefits.

'I'm a full-time carer for my youngest Christina, who is disabled. It was awful not being able to live like a proper family.

I was having sleepless nights and spent the whole time worrying and feeling sick.

'We got constant hassle. Nasty letters and phone calls demanding money. Lloyds TSB were the worst. They bombarded us with letters, calls at home and messages on my mobile. It was hell.'

After eight years, just trying to pay for the essentials, Lorraine and Dave ended up owing £30,000 on a bank overdraft, various credit cards, loans and a catalogue club. Lorraine was at her wits' end.

'At my absolute rock bottom I felt like ending it all. I kept thinking if I was gone the debts would be gone, too, and the kids would be OK. That was the only way I could see out of this terrible mess.'

Lorraine eventually went to her local Citizens Advice Bureau for help. The bureau's adviser explained the options available to Lorraine and Dave, including declaring bankruptcy.

As they were keen to repay their debts the adviser helped Lorraine draw up a budget and work out a debt management plan that they could afford. Part of the plan included a freeze on debt interest so that all their monthly repayments reduced the outstanding debt. The adviser also made sure they received all the state financial benefits they were entitled to.

After working out the plan with the money adviser Lorraine and her family got their lives back. 'We are all living together as one happy family and can see a day when we will finally be debt-free,' she said.

Source: Adapted from '£30K in debt: But finally, we're sorting it out'. Mirror Online (2012)

Help through your employer

Depending on the size of your employer, they might provide access to personal finance related help and guidance such as:

- Financial well-being insights, education, reminders and alerts via text, email, or app alerts on key factors that can help you improve your financial well-being.
- Unsecured loans and savings accounts provided by specialist companies, based on and administered through your employer's payroll.
- Group presentations on pensions and/or general financial well-being provided either in house or by outside providers.
- One-to-one help from the human resources or pension department to explain benefits, options and key choices.
- Access to a personalised financial coaching service, delivered either face-to-face or via video conferencing, either fully paid for or subsidised by your employer.
- A panel of regulated financial advice firms that are familiar with your company's benefit package and that meet certain minimum criteria, although you will usually have to pay any fees.
- Provision of tax-free financial advice vouchers of up to £500 per annum, either as an additional benefit or by you giving up a corresponding amount of salary (to avoid income tax and National Insurance) to help fund financial advice.

How to choose the right help

One way to work out what type of help you might need and benefit from is to carry out a simple online healthcheck assessment. The following tool will help you to identify which areas of your financial life need looking at: www.moneyadviceservice.org.uk/en/tools/health-check.

If your needs are simple and modest then you can probably deal with any actions yourself. If, however, your needs are more complex or the numbers more substantial, you might benefit from seeking more personalised advice.

Figure 8.4 will help you to work out what your main need is and to identify from what type of help you would get most value.

What help do I need?	
Need	Type of help
General awareness and education about money matters	Employer provided financial well-being portal and alerts Personal finance website, books and presentations
Help demystifying money, reducing money anxieties and learning how to use money effectively	Personal money coaching Personal financial life planning
Help understanding financial options as you approach retirement (aged 50+)	Government funded Pension Wise* service (phone or face-to-face)
General help with basic financial issues	Free government money advice service (web or phone)
Personal advice on more complex issues such as pension transfers, mortgages, investing, pension funding, general financial planning, long-term care funding	Authorised and regulated financial adviser (face-to-face, digital or video conferencing)
Assistance to help you work out how to invest modest amounts for the long term, such as a stocks and shares individual savings account (ISA)	Online investment guidance* service (this is NOT personalised financial planning advice)
Problem debt	Free debt advice charities such as Citizens Advice* and StepChange*

Figure 8.4 What help do I need?

Source: Author's categorisation

Barriers to regulated advice

One piece of research (Moss, 2013) found that the three main reasons why people don't access the financial advice they need are:

- Knowledge level: of both the need for advice and the type of advice available
- Trust level: in both in the financial sector generally and the individual adviser
- Affordability and price: the willingness or ability to pay for advice and perceived value from doing so.

Providing personal financial advice in the UK is subject to very strict regulation. Advisers must hold certain professional qualifications and undertake ongoing training. The adviser has to find out about the client's circumstances in order to provide 'suitable' advice and recommendations. These high standards have inevitably led to a reduction in the number of advisers and a rise in the cost of advice over the past decade.

As set out in Figure 8.2 earlier, there are a range of options for people seeking help with their finances and not all of them involve regulated, personalised (and usually face-to-face) financial advice.

The Financial Conduct Authority* regulates financial advice in the UK and it had this to say about the role of regulated advice (FCA, 2016):

> A number of factors combine to mean that not all consumers can currently afford to access the advice they need at a price they are willing or able to pay. The market currently delivers high-quality solutions to those who can afford advice. However, not everyone wants or needs a personal recommendation in respect of every decision, nor do they always need a comprehensive assessment of all of their financial circumstances and requirements.

The conclusion, therefore, is that sometimes generic guidance or advice which focuses on one area or issue can be perfectly adequate and preferential to not seeking help. In this regard financial therapy, financial life planning or financial guidance could be a good place to start.

Figure 8.5 sets out the key differences between financial guidance and personalised financial advice which is provided by a regulated financial services firm.

How to choose the right adviser

There are several useful directories that can help you find a potential adviser and the main ones are listed in Table 8.1.

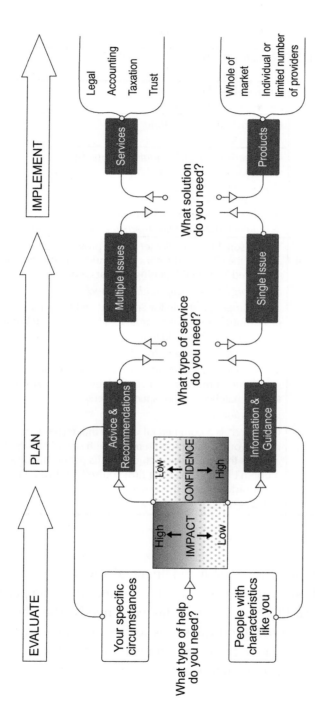

Figure 8.5 The difference between financial guidance and advice

Source: Jason Butler (2014). Reproduced by permission of the author

Table 8.1 Choosing the right adviser

What sort of help do you want?	Examples of where to find it
Money therapy*	*financial-coaching.co.uk* *moneycoachinginstitute.com*
Financial life planning*	*kinderinstitute.com/planner-search/*
Debt advice*	*citizensadvice.org.uk/about-us/contact-us/* *web-chat-service-mas/* *stepchange.org* *mymoneysteps.org* *payplan.com/free-online-debt-help* *debtadvicefoundation.org/personal-debt-analyser*
Authorised and regulated personal financial advice	The Personal Finance Society is the professional body that awards the Chartered Financial Planner qualification and Chartered Financial Planning Firm accreditation. *thepfs.org/membership/findanadviser/* The Chartered Institute for Securities and Investment* is the professional body that awards both the Chartered Wealth Manager and Certified Financial Planner accreditation. *financialplanning.org.uk/wayfinder/find-planner* Vouched for* is a commercial website that enables you to search for a firm based on verified reviews by existing customers matched to your specific needs. *vouchedfor.co.uk* Unbiased* is a commercial website that enables you to match your specific requirements with one of the regulated advisers that pay to be included on its panel. The downside is it doesn't let you choose a firm yourself, and you have to wait for the adviser to contact you. *unbiased.co.uk*

If you are looking for a regulated financial adviser, it's a good idea to create a shortlist of three potential firms and then compare them to find the one that you feel best fits your needs. The checklist in Table 8.2 gives some good questions to pose to each firm, so you can compare their answers. If any firm isn't keen to take the time to answer these questions, that is a good indication that they aren't a good firm.

Table 8.2 Financial adviser selection checklist

	Criteria	Your notes
1	Do you advise people like me/am I the type of client you are looking for?	
2	Do you offer a one off financial check-up or do I need to commit to an ongoing service – and if so how long is that commitment?	
3	How much time will I need to spend working with you and what will this involve?	
4	How can you make my life easier and less stressful in relation to money?	
5	Who in your firm will be working on my affairs and interacting with me on a day-to-day basis (i.e. just you or a number of colleagues)?	
6	Exactly how are your charges calculated and how do you minimise and manage any potential conflict of interests?	
7	How will I know I am getting good value for money from using your service and how will we monitor and review this on an ongoing basis?	
8	Can I speak to a few of your existing long-standing clients who have a similar profile to me?	
9	Please confirm that you are a Chartered or Accredited Financial Planning firm and provide your registration number.	
10	Do you have a network of complementary other experts, such as legal, accounting, tax planning, that you can call on and liaise with as necessary?	
11	Please provide me with a simple overview of how you deliver your advice (including overall financial planning and investment philosophy).	
12	Please confirm that your firm is regulated by the UK Financial Conduct Authority (including registration number) and whether your firm has had any complaints upheld by the Financial Ombudsman Service in the past three years.	

Source: Author's checklist

What to do if things go wrong

All regulated firms have a complaints procedure which they must follow. In the first instance, if you are unhappy with the advice or service provided, you should raise the matter with the firm. The firm must respond to your complaint in writing within a certain timeframe.

If you are unhappy with the firm's response, then you can take your complaint to the Financial Ombudsman Service* (FOS). This is a free service for consumers, funded by a levy on regulated firms.

FOS has the power to investigate complaints against regulated advice firms and can compel a financial firm to pay fair compensation up to £150,000 plus any costs and interest.

A financial award from FOS doesn't preclude you from taking legal action against a firm. You may need to do this if you are seeking financial compensation which is in excess of the FOS maximum.

If a UK financial firm goes out of business and has insufficient assets to pay financial claims against it, the Financial Services Compensation Scheme* (FSCS) is the official body that provides financial compensation to customers. It is funded by a levy paid each year by UK authorised financial services firms.

Table 8.3 shows the compensation limits for the main types of financial products for new claims (different limits may apply for earlier claims depending on the category).

Table 8.3 Financial Services Compensation Scheme limits

Type of financial product	Maximum compensation	Notes
Deposit accounts	100% of first the £85,000 per person, per financial firm	Up to £1m is protected if it is a temporary balance that arose from one of a range of qualifying transactions e.g. sale of a property or inheritance
Home finance	Up to £50,000 per person per firm	In relation to the advice and arrangement of a mortgage
Investment funds	Up to £50,000 per person per firm	This doesn't include normal market losses that relate to investments which were judged suitable and appropriate

Table 8.3 Continued

Type of financial product	Maximum compensation	Notes
Long-term insurance including life, sickness and guaranteed annuities	100% of the benefit is protected, without limit	Some forms of long-term insurance are protected up to 90% of the benefit
General insurance advice and arranging	90% of the claim is protected unless it is compulsory insurance, which is 100% protected	Includes things like motor, property and travel insurance

Source: Author's table based on information from Financial Services Compensation Scheme

Conclusion

Your employer will make certain financial plans for you, such as basic pension contributions and possibly other benefits such as life and sickness insurance. But there is also a wealth of useful and free personal finance help and support available to you, both online and via your employer, to help you make better financial decisions.

There is much you can and should do for yourself in relation to your money, but don't be afraid to seek personal coaching, guidance or regulated advice if you feel out of your depth or lack the time and inclination to make the best decisions. The cost of taking advice needs to be compared to the cost of not taking it and the value of your time spent trying to figure things out for yourself.

If you do want and need more personalised help and advice, you can have confidence that the UK has one of the best regulated, most professional financial services sectors in the world. Professional standards of advice are higher than they have ever been, most financial firms are managed far more professionally than in the past, and innovation in products and services continues apace.

If you do experience poor advice or a financial company can't meet its obligations to you, in most cases you will be fully protected and compensated.

References

Butler, J. (2014) *The Financial Times Guide to Wealth Management* (second edition). Prentice Hall.

Engelmann, J., Capra, C., Noussair, C., and Berns, G. (2009) 'Expert financial advice neurobiologically "offloads" decision-making under risk'. *PLoS ONE*, 4(3): e4957.

Financial Conduct Authority (2016) *Financial Advice Market Review – Final Report* [online] www.fca.org.uk/publication/corporate/famr-final-report.pdf (accessed 23 September 2018).

Financial Services Compensation Scheme (2018) www.fscs.org.uk/your-claim/compensation-limits/ (accessed 31 March 2018).

Kinder Institute (2018) 'Financial consumers' [online] www.kinderinstitute.com/public/ (accessed 30 March 2018).

Mirror Online (2012) '£30K in debt: but finally, we're sorting it out'. 3 February [online] www.mirror.co.uk/money/personal-finance/30k-in-debt-298585 (accessed 12 March 2018).

Moss, J. (2013) Unpublished PhD thesis 'Personal financial planning advice: barriers to access' [online] http://etheses.bham.ac.uk/6016/1/Moss15PhD.pdf (accessed 16 March 2018).

Somers, M. (2018) *Advice that Sticks: How to Give Financial Advice that People Will Follow*. Practical Inspiration Publishing.

Steffel, M., Williams, E. and Perrmann-Graham, J. (2016) 'Passing the buck: delegating choices to others to avoid responsibility and blame'. *Organizational Behavior and Human Decision Processes*, 135: 32–44.

Online courses

Open University: *Managing My Money* at www.open.edu/openlearn/money-management/managing-my-money/content-section-overview.

Open University: *Managing My Money – Young Adults* at www.open.edu/openlearn/money-business/managing-my-money-young-adults/content-section-overview.

Open University: *Managing My Investments* at www.open.edu/openlearn/money-management/managing-my-investments/content-section-overview?active-tab=description-tab.

Conclusion
9 | Jonquil Lowe

In a nutshell:

- **Benefits from work, not just pay, can help you reach your goals.**
- **Knowing yourself can help you achieve goals and live happily.**
- **No-one has a crystal ball – you are not at fault if things don't go quite to plan.**

We are all individuals, so your particular life goals will be different from those of your neighbour. That said, you have seen as this book unfolded how we typically have some broad goals in common. These include, for example, protecting our loved ones, making ourselves resilient to shocks like unexpected bills or job loss, and having some income to live on when eventually we cut back on or stop work. The package of pay and benefits you get from work can help you achieve these goals.

How work helps you reach your goals

Clearly your pay is the most valuable reward from work and is the engine that drives your financial well-being. It enables you to spend today on the things you need and want, to pay off debts built up in the past and to save in order to achieve future goals. But pay is not the only reward from work.

Benefits in kind

Your job may come with a kaleidoscope of other non-pay benefits, called 'benefits in kind', that can also help with your financial planning. Many are included in Figure 9.1.

The practice of employers providing benefits in kind has a variety of origins. Pensions can be traced back hundreds of years and were a way of compassionately retiring workers who were no longer fit enough to work. In the Victorian era, some employers – such as Cadbury, Lever Brothers, Clarks and Rowntree – adopted a paternalistic

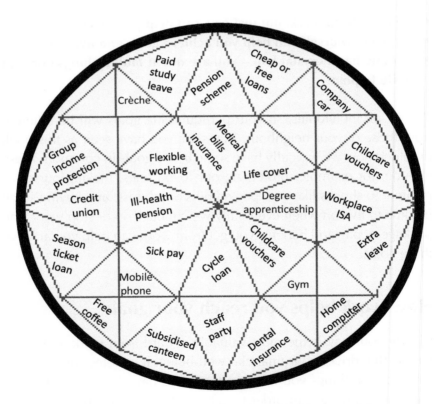

Figure 9.1 A kaleidoscope of benefits in kind from your job

Source: Author's diagram

approach towards their employees, providing for example housing with good sanitation, community facilities, sick pay and accident benefits. To some extent, employee benefits were displaced when the National Health Service and welfare state were established from 1948 onwards. However, benefits in kind are a way for employers to attract and retain staff and became especially important in 1970s Britain when the government restrained pay increases in an effort to contain high rates of inflation. Once established within a firm, it can be hard to take benefits away and so they continue to be an integral part of many remuneration packages.

Many benefits in kind have been discussed in the preceding chapters of this book. To recap, they may include help with, for example:

- Increasing the value of your human capital. Your workplace may offer in-house training, sponsorship to take external qualifications or paid study leave. This may help you progress your career with your current employer, but often also equips you with transferable skills that enable you to move to other jobs that pay more and/or let you do the work you find most satisfying. Since April 2017, larger employers have, by law, to pay an apprenticeship levy. This is a tax but employers can get the levy back if they offer apprenticeships through the workplace. These are not limited to new recruits and can include high-level qualifications, such as degree apprenticeships (that mix workplace and university study).
- Turning your human capital into income by, for example, providing a workplace crèche or (for parents already receiving them) childcare vouchers. (However, the tax-free childcare voucher has been replaced since 2017 by a new government childcare savings scheme, called Tax-Free Childcare*; but employees who started getting childcare vouchers from their employer before 6 October 2018 can continue to get them.) Flexible working and paid time off for caring emergencies can also help to make it easier to manage caring responsibilities while pursuing a rewarding career.
- Saving for retirement. Now that automatic enrolment into a workplace pension scheme has been rolled out across all UK employers,

most employees are automatically made members of a retirement savings scheme and employers must contribute towards this.

- Protecting your family in the event of death. Either as part of the pension scheme or separately, most employers offer some type of death-in-service benefit or life insurance. As you saw earlier, commonly there might be a lump sum payment of between two and four times your salary at the time of death. The pension scheme may also pay either a lump sum or pensions for a surviving partner and/or children.
- Saving and borrowing. Some workplaces have credit unions or the option to put some of your pay directly into an Individual Savings Account (ISA) which can help you save regularly, for example, to build up an emergency fund. Credit unions can also be a source of affordable loans. Your employer might offer free or cheap loans for other purposes, such as buying a season ticket for travel to work.
- Protecting your human capital. By law, employers must provide at least a minimum amount of sick pay under the statutory sick pay scheme. Many employers run their own more generous schemes. If health problems or disability mean you have to stop work early, you may qualify for an ill-health pension. Some employers offer private medical insurance and dental insurance which may help to minimise your time off work.

Figure 9.2 shows the results of a survey by the Chartered Institute of Personnel and Development (2018) which found that the availability and take-up of some common benefits both vary. Its research also found that (excluding pensions) the benefits that are valued most by employees are healthcare and health insurances.

Action point: Make sure you know what non-pay benefits are available in your workplace and consider which could help you manage your money and reach your goals.

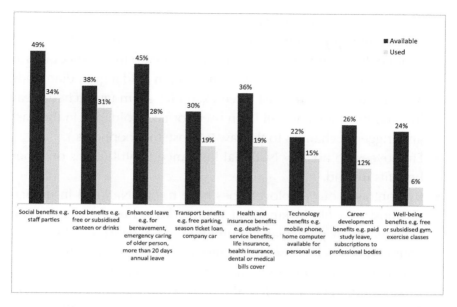

Figure 9.2 Most common non-pay benefits and extent to which they are used

Source: Author's chart using data from CIPD (2018)

Note: The base is 4,985 employees from a sample that is representative of the UK workforce.

Flexible benefits

Often workplaces let you choose what benefits in kind you'd like to have. Your workplace may have a menu of benefits and you can select the ones that are relevant and valuable for you personally. For example, if you're a parent, help with childcare costs and flexible working might seem particularly attractive. Others might prefer, say, extra paid holiday, gym membership or enhanced contributions to the pension scheme.

How benefits are taxed

It's important to bear in mind that receiving benefits in kind can affect the amount of tax you pay. The general rules are:

- You pay income tax and National Insurance contributions on your pay (wages, salary, overtime, and so on).

- Any benefits that can be easily turned into cash are taxed like pay and so subject to income tax and National Insurance. This would capture, for example, being given a credit card that you could use for your personal spending or being paid in gold ingots, diamonds and fine wines! (If the last three examples seem far-fetched, bear in mind that they have all been used for tax avoidance in the past and triggered changes to the law to close the loopholes.)
- Employees do not pay National Insurance contributions on other benefits in kind.
- By contrast, your employer does have to pay National Insurance on most benefits in kind that it provides – but there are some exceptions, in particular contributions to a pension scheme on your behalf, cycle-to-work schemes and childcare vouchers.
- Employees do have to pay income tax on the value of benefits in kind they receive, unless the benefits are specifically tax-free. Table 9.1 gives a list of the most common tax-free benefits.

Table 9.1 Common tax-free benefits in kind

Your employer's goods and services	If free or discounted they are tax-free; provided there is no cost to your employer. Examples include getting goods at the wholesale price, free train travel if you work for a train company (provided you don't displace a fare-paying passenger).
Travel	Tax-free mileage allowance if you use your car for work up to a specified limit (40p per mile for the first 10,000 miles and a lower rate above that) even if the actual cost to you of your business mileage is less.
	Free parking at work.
	Cycle-to-work schemes: loan of a bicycle and related safety equipment for cycling between home and work, even if you use it for private journeys as well.
Financial	Employer contributions to a pension scheme on your behalf.
	Life insurance.
	Cheap or free loans provided the total is no more than £10,000.
	Pension advice arranged by your employer up to the value of £500 a year.

Table 9.1 Continued

Childcare	Nursery or crèche at work (whatever the value of this benefit).
	Childcare vouchers to buy 'approved' childcare (e.g. in a nursery or with a registered childminder) up to a maximum value of £55 a week for basic-rate taxpayers but less if you're taxed at a higher rate
Other	Free or subsidised food, hot drinks and water at work provided available to all employees (and not in a public restaurant).
	Mobile phone.
	Annual health check-up.

Source: Author's table based on data from various government sources, for example GOV.uk (nda).

Benefits that are not specifically tax-free are taxable. Taxable benefits include for example private medical insurance, a company car, gym membership, accommodation unless it's necessary for doing your job (say, you're a caretaker) and, in most cases, items that your employer gives you. The principle behind them being taxable is that they are for – or potentially available for – your private use. Some use you might not think of as private is considered by the tax authority to be your own personal use, such as commuting between home and your workplace.

There are special rules for working out the value you are deemed to get from a taxable benefit in kind. If you receive taxable benefits, your employer will give you a form (called a P11D) once a year telling you their taxable value, and you may need to fill in a tax return. The value of the benefits will be added to your income for the year when tax is worked out.

Ryan's story

Ryan's employer provides him with a company car. It's a 1.5 litre petrol Audi A3 which emits 116g of carbon dioxide (CO_2) per kilometre, costing £28,000. The CO_2 emissions and list price determine the taxable value of the car. The taxable value of this car in 2018–19 is £6,720. Ryan is a higher-rate taxpayer so has to pay £2,688 (40% × £6,720) extra in income tax as a result of having the company car.

Action point: If your employer lets you choose a company car, before deciding check out what its taxable value will be using the government's company car tax calculator* at http://cccfcalculator.hmrc.gov.uk/CCF2.aspx.

Salary sacrifice

Flexible benefits are often linked to **salary sacrifice** schemes. This is where you agree to a contractual reduction in your pay and get an increase in non-pay benefits instead. Salary sacrifice became popular because of the different way in which pay and tax-free benefits are taxed. However, the government has recently clamped down on salary sacrifice schemes, restricting the tax savings to just this narrow range of benefits (HMRC, 2016):

- employer pension contributions
- employer-provided pension advice
- cycle-to-work schemes
- childcare vouchers
- ultra-low-emission vehicles.

The idea behind salary sacrifice is that you swap some pay on which you're charged income tax and National Insurance for a tax-free benefit in kind on which there is no tax or National Insurance. In the case of the narrow range of benefits listed above, your employer also saves on National insurance and might be willing to share some of those savings with you.

Bear in mind that there has to be a genuine change to your contract so that you are paid less. This means that anything related to your salary, such as sick pay and maternity pay, will also be reduced. On the other hand, lower pay could mean you qualify for means-tested work-related benefits, such as tax credits and **universal credit** (or an increased amount if you're already claiming these).

You are not allowed to sacrifice so much pay that what remains is less than the national living wage (which is £7.83 per hour in 2018–19 if you're aged 25 or over, increasing to £8.21 in 2019–20) (GOV.uk, ndb).

Building on help from work

Aim to make the most of any benefits in kind available from work; they can help you on your way to achieving your goals. But, valuable as these benefits are, in many cases they will only take you so far. As you've seen in the preceding chapters, help from your employer and (typically to a lesser extent) from the state provide a foundation on which to build by reducing the resources you personally need to find to achieve your goals. It's like a sum:

Your goals – Any help from state and employer = Amount left for you to fund privately

You can think of achieving your goals as like climbing a staircase (see Figure 9.3). In effect as you climb the 'goals staircase', help from your employer and (mainly in the case of pensions) the state makes each tread less deep and the whole staircase easier to climb. Moreover, they mean you have more income left to set against these and other goals.

Know yourself

Chapters 2 to 7 have described the types of planning and financial products that you use to fill any gap that remains after employer and

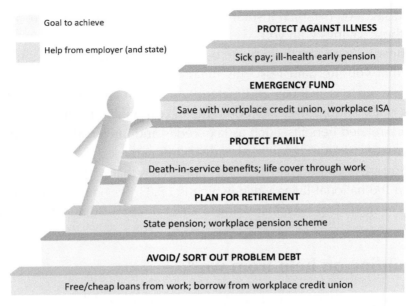

Figure 9.3 Benefits from work make it easier to achieve your goals
Source: Author's chart

state support are taken into account. But the ultimate key to achieving well-being is to be found in Chapter 1. It's about knowing yourself and your relationship with money. Having too little money and especially being in debt creates stress, worry and depression, but beyond a certain amount money does not create happiness. As far as possible, shift away from comparing yourself with others and focus on what gives you personally greatest joy. Time with your family, voluntary work, feeling part of a community may ultimately give you greater satisfaction than wringing every last pound from your human capital.

Nevertheless, you need to strike a healthy balance between living well today and planning to ensure your future is equally secure and happy. You have seen throughout this book how our natural behavioural traits often skew the way we view life. We don't like to contemplate bad events like getting ill or dying or the reality that we will one day become old. It's much more pleasant not to dwell on such gloomy thoughts, but such a fair-weather perspective is dangerous. It leaves you and those who you are close to exposed to life events. Being aware of this natural inclination to close one's eyes to what might, could or will happen is the essential first step to doing something about it.

Running your own life is a bit like running a business. You've already used some tools to look at your finances that are common in business when you looked at budgeting and the capital you have available, both human and financial. You might like to think about other techniques that perhaps you use at work and how these could be applied to 'You plc', such as:

- SWOT analysis (identifying strengths, weaknesses, opportunities and threats). Applying this analysis to yourself will sharpen your awareness of what stands in the way of achieving your goals and the planning that will enable you to overcome such obstacles.
- Scenario planning. Many businesses these days think through 'what if?' scenarios to identify threats or to consider the range of possible outcomes from an action. This same approach is in effect the basis of determining what insurance or savings you need to build into your financial plan.
- Project planning. Big goals, like planning for a secure retirement or buying a home cannot be achieved overnight and can seem daunting. Break down what's required into stages with achievable timescales – for example, the amount you will save each month, interim targets – and celebrate the milestones. Put in place devices to make positive outcomes more likely, such as setting up standing orders to commit yourself to saving the amounts you intended.
- Annual report and accounts. Get into the habit of once a year of reviewing the financial situation of You plc. It's a reality check to see if your finances are on an improving or worsening trend, and whether you are on track for the goals you have set. You should also go through this review exercise whenever there are major changes in your life or external events – like a major tax change or rise in interest rates – that could affect you.

Conclusion

This book brings together many ideas, guidance, tips and suggested actions. We hope it will be an inspiration and also provide answers to some of those niggly questions we all have about money matters. And that it will help you to organise your money and plan ahead more effectively.

Overall, though, our advice is: be kind to yourself. Nobody knows everything; and there is no crystal ball to tell us what the future holds. For good times and rocky times, there are many sources of help available as described in Chapter 8, so you should never feel you have to struggle alone. Life is full of surprises, both good and bad. It will be rare for life or your goals to proceed exactly as you had planned. But the approaches described in this book will help you to weather the unexpected, avoid the worst and – best of all – achieve at least some of your dreams.

References

Chartered Institute of Personnel and Development (CIPD) (2018) *UK Working Lives. The CIPD Job Quality Index* [online] www.cipd.co.uk/knowledge/work/trends/uk-working-lives (accessed 17 June 2018).

GOV.uk (nda) *Expenses and benefits: A to Z* [online] www.gov.uk/expenses-and-benefits-a-to-z (accessed 17 June 2018).

GOV.uk (ndb) *National Minimum Wage and National Living Wage rates* [online] www.gov.uk/national-minimum-wage-rates (accessed 17 June 2018).

HMRC (2016) *Income tax: Limitation of Salary Sacrifice.* Policy paper [online] www.gov.uk/government/publications/income-tax-limitation-of-salary-sacrifice/income-tax-limitation-of-salary-sacrifice (accessed 17 June 2018).

Glossary

Accident, sickness and unemployment (ASU) insurance A short-term insurance policy that pays out an income in the event of accident, sickness or involuntary unemployment.

Active fund Refers to a fund which relies on the input from a fund manager to decide on what shares to buy, sell and hold.

Active income (also called earned income) Income you receive for the work you do.

Additional voluntary contribution (AVC) scheme A tax-advantaged arrangement available through work that lets you top up your saving for retirement. You employer might partially or fully match the amount you pay in.

Anchoring Refers to the tendency to make judgements relative to an initial piece of information.

Annuity An arrangement where you use part or all of your pot of savings to buy an income. With a lifetime annuity, the income is payable for the rest of your life, however long you live, and so is a type of insurance that protects you against longevity risk.

Artificial intelligence The use of computers to replicate intelligent human behaviour. This may include machine learning where the system automatically adapts in the light of experience gained.

Asset An item that you own. Usually interpreted as something you hold because you expect it to maintain or increase its value (though the value of many assets can fall as well as rise).

Authorised overdraft An arrangement you have agreed in advance with your bank to borrow from it by spending more money than you have in your current account.

Automatically enrolled Being placed into a pension scheme at work without your prior consent, but with the choice of opting out.

Benefits in kind Non-cash forms of remuneration from work.

Bereavement benefit A benefit paid by the government to the surviving husband, wife or civil partner (but not unmarried partner) of a person who dies provided certain contribution conditions are met.

Bereavement support payment An income paid by the government to the surviving husband, wife or civil partner (but not unmarried partner) of a person who dies provided certain contribution conditions are met.

Bond A type of investment in which an investor loans money to an organisation (typically company or government) for a period of time and usually receives a regular income in return. Usually, bonds can be bought and sold on the stock market rather than being held for the full term.

Budget A detailed statement of future income and spending that is a fundamental tool for controlling and planning your finances.

Buy-to-let A property that is purchased to rent out to others rather than to live in yourself.

Capital expenditure Spending on items that are expected to be usable for a number of years.

Capital loss The loss or depreciation in value of the amount of money invested.

Career average scheme A type of pension scheme where you are promised a specified level of pension worked out as a fraction of your pay average over the whole time you've been in the scheme.

Cash reserve Another name for an *emergency fund* (see below).

Cashflow The current or expected money you have coming in and the money you spend over a specified period of time, often listed in a statement or summarised in a chart to help you see your current financial situation and the impact of financial decisions.

Compound interest Refers to the interest paid on the initial sum of money invested as well as interest paid on the amount of interest you have accumulated.

Contactless payment A way of making small payments that uses radio frequencies to communicate between your plastic card, smart phone or other device and the payment terminal.

Council tax An annual tax based on the value of the property you live in.

Credit card A means of paying for items or drawing out cash initially using borrowed money. You choose whether to pay off all of the sum each month or pay just part and continue borrowing the rest.

Credit reference agencies (CRAs) Organisations that hold personal and financial data about almost every adult in the UK that is used by lenders to check the creditworthiness of potential customers.

Credit score A numerical indicator of creditworthiness. Although credit reference agencies often provide indicative scores, in reality each lender works out its own score for you when deciding whether or not to lend to you and how much to charge.

Credit union An organisation that provides a savings account, loans and sometimes other financial products too for a group of people who are linked by some common bond, such as working for the same employer.

Critical illness cover A health insurance policy that pays out on diagnosis of a life-threatening illness (such as stroke, cancer).

Death in service benefit A type of life insurance provided by your employer for free.

Debit card A plastic card that you can use to pay for things where the payment comes direct from your bank account.

Defined-benefit scheme A type of pension arrangement where you are promised a specified level of pension, often related to your salary while working.

Defined-contribution scheme A type of pension arrangement where you build up your own personal pot of savings that you can use later on to provide yourself with a retirement income (or use in other ways if you choose).

Direct debit Arrangement where you give permission to a supplier of goods or services you're buying to take money direct from your account to pay your bill with that supplier.

Disability benefit Income that is paid by the government to someone who is unable to work due to sickness, illness or a medical condition.

Discretionary expenses Spending which is not essential.

Dividend tax allowance (DTA) (also called dividend allowance) Allows you to have up to £2,000 a year (in 2018–19) of income from dividends free from income tax.

Dividends Name given to the income from *equities* (see below).

Drawdown An arrangement where you leave your pension savings invested but have the option to draw an income and or lump sums direct from these savings.

Emergency fund A pot of savings you build up so that you can draw on it if you become financially stressed due to, say, a drop in income or an unexpected bill.

Employment and Support Allowance (ESA) A benefit paid for a period of time to those who have paid enough National Insurance contributions when they cannot work due to illness or disability.

Endowment mortgage An *interest-only mortgage* (see below) combined with an endowment policy that has the same term. The aim is that the endowment policy will pay out a lump sum at the end of the term which is enough to pay off the mortgage, though this is usually not guaranteed.

Endowment policy A type of life insurance, typically used mainly as an investment, that is designed to pay out a cash lump sum either on death or at the end of a specified term, whichever happens first.

Equities Investments where in effect you become part-owner of the company that issues them. Your return depends on the profitability of the company, the extent to which profits are paid out to investors (as dividends) and how other investors rate the prospects of the company (which determine the price of the equities on the stock market).

Estate The value of everything you own less everything you owe, particularly at the date of death.

Family income benefit A type of life insurance that pays out an income (rather than lump sum) to the family of the deceased person for a fixed period of time.

Final salary scheme A type of pension scheme where you are promised a specified level of pension worked out as a fraction of your pay close to retirement and the length of time you've been in the scheme.

Financial advice Usually means recommendations from a professional person or firm, regulated by the Financial Conduct Authority, to buy products or take other actions deemed suitable for you and your particular circumstances.

Financial capability Refers to the knowledge, skills, attitudes and behaviours that enable you to manage money well, day-to-day, by planning ahead and through significant life events and periods of financial difficulty.

Financial capital The value today of the assets you've accumulated (such as investments, pensions and property).

Financial freedom Closely related to *financial independence* (see below), this refers to a situation when you can decide what to do and how you wish to spend your time without worrying about money.

Financial independence The ability to fund your desired lifestyle throughout any stage of life regardless of your ability or desire to work.

Financial life planning A consultative approach based on the premise that each person needs to discover their essential goals in life before they go on to formulate a financial plan to support those goals.

Financial planning The process of determining whether and how you can meet your life goals through the effective management of your financial resources.

Freedom and choice A UK government policy introduced from April 2015 onwards that allows you to use the proceeds of a defined-contribution scheme for any purpose (not just providing yourself with retirement income), provided you have reached a minimum age (currently 55).

General insurance Most types of insurance other than those relating to life and health, for example motor and home insurance, pet insurance, and so on.

Generic information Used to refer to knowledge, explanations, data and other information that could help you to make informed decisions but is not tailored to your own particular situation.

Gilts A type of bond, that can be bought and sold on the stock market, where you are lending money to the UK government usually in return for a regular income.

Guidance An indication of courses of action that could be suitable for anyone meeting the broad criteria specified but not tailored to your own particular situation.

Herding The tendency by an individual to copy actions of a larger group.

Hire purchase (HP) Arrangement that has been common for many decades, where you buy household appliances, furniture, a car or other items, getting to use them straight away but paying for them by regular monthly instalments.

Human capital The value today of all your potential future earnings. Human capital can be increased, for example, through education, training and experience, but tends to decline after a certain age as remaining working life shrinks.

Illegal lender (also called a loan shark) A lender who is not authorised by the Financial Conduct Authority and so breaking the law by lending to you. Such lenders usually charge very high interest rates and often use threatening or violent tactics to get the money you owe them.

Illiquid Assets (e.g. such as property) which are not easily converted into cash. Sometimes extended to also mean assets that can be turned into cash but, since their price is volatile, you cannot be sure how much cash you will get.

Income protection insurance (also known as permanent health insurance) A type of health insurance designed to provide a replacement income if you are unable to work because of illness or disability.

Individual savings account (ISA) A tax-advantaged way of saving where you can put your money into savings accounts or investments.

Inertia Refers to tendency of beliefs to persist once formed or a tendency to put off actions indefinitely even if they are recognised as important.

Inflation risk The chance that the buying power of your income or a lump sum will fall in future because of a permanent rise in prices.

Inheritance tax A tax on the value of your *estate* (see above) when you die and, in some cases, gifts made in the seven years before death.

Insurance Financial products that pay out compensation if a specified event (usually unwelcome) occurs.

Interest The return you get from a savings account (or some types of investment). Alternatively, a cost you pay when you borrow money.

Interest-only mortgage A type of *mortgage* (see below) where your monthly payments pay off only the interest. At the end of the term, you still owe and must repay the amount you originally borrowed.

Investment return The profit from investing in an *asset* (see above), which may comprise income, a rise (or fall) in value, or both.

Investment risk The possibility that the value of your investments will be worth less than you had expected or less than the amount you need to achieve your goals.

Investments Assets whose value can go up and down. These may be 'tangible' assets (also called 'real' assets), such as a house or gold bar, or 'intangible' assets such as *equities* (see above).

Liabilities Things that you owe to others, such as money borrowed, tax owed and bills due for services already used.

Life assurance (often just called life insurance) An insurance that will definitely pay out a sum of money, which may be on the death of the person whose life is insured or at the end of a specified time.

Life cover Type of insurance that pays out a lump sum or income if the insured person dies.

Life expectancy The period of time a person is expected to continue living.

Life insurance A financial product that pays out a lump sum (or sometimes an income) if the insured person dies during a specified period of time.

Lifetime allowance charge Extra income tax that you must pay in any year if (broadly speaking) the cumulative total drawn out of your pension savings (including death benefits paid out) exceeds a specified amount.

Long term Typically refers to a period of time of ten years or more.

Longevity risk The chance that you may live longer than expected and so perhaps outlive any savings you depend on for income.

Loss aversion Refers to people's tendency to prefer avoiding losses to acquiring equivalent gains.

Lump sum term assurance A life policy that pays out an amount of money (once) rather than a regular income.

Medium term Typically refers to a period of time of 5–10 years

Money coaching A form of therapy that combines psychology, financial education and support, to help people make better financial decisions.

Money pools Arrangements where a group of people regularly pay money into a pool and take turns to receive the accumulated lump sum.

Money purchase scheme Another name for a defined-contribution scheme (see entry above).

Mortgage A loan secured against your home, typically used to buy that home. 'Secured' means you could lose your home if you do not keep up the payments.

Mortgage interest support A government loan scheme to help home-owners on a low income pay their mortgage interest. (Previously, this was a state benefit rather than a loan.)

Mortgage payment protection insurance (MPPI) A short-term insurance policy that pays out an income to you to enable you to meet your mortgage payment and other associated costs if you are sick or lose your job.

Myopia A behavioural trait where you tend to ignore what might happen in the future and focus only on today.

Myopic A tendency to ignore the future and instead focus just on today.

National Insurance A compulsory tax paid by employers, employees and the self-employed that builds entitlement to claim specified state benefits during periods of unemployment, inability to work due to illness, bereavement and retirement. People who cannot work because of caring responsibilities or illness may be credited as if they have paid the tax.

Occupational pension (also called company schemes or superannuation). A workplace pension scheme run by your employer.

Occupational sick pay (OSP) An income provided by employers to employees who are unable to work due to sickness.

Passive fund An investment approach where you invest in a market index, rather than a fund chosen by a fund manager.

Passive income Income you receive on a regular basis with no or minimal work.

Payday loan An expensive form of short-term borrowing.

Pension A regular income designed to support you after you stop work in later life.

Pension commencement lump sum (PCLS) The technical name for a tax-free lump sum you draw from a pension scheme at the point when you are ready to start a retirement income.

Pension scheme A tax-advantaged way of saving for retirement.

Permanent health insurance See income protection insurance above.

Personal contract purchase (PCP) An arrangement where you lease a car (rather than buying it) for a specified period. At the end of the period, you typically have the option of paying a lump sum to buy the car outright, switching the leasing deal to a new car, or stopping than plan in which case you no longer have a car.

Personal Independence Payment A state benefit to help with the extra costs of living as a result of a long-term health condition or a disability.

Personal loan A loan, usually from a bank, that you can use for any purpose. It may be secured against your home or other assets, but more often is an *unsecured loan* (see below).

Personal pension A pension scheme, typically run by an insurance company or investment firm, that may be a workplace pension or a pension that you arrange for yourself.

Personal savings allowance (PSA) Allows many taxpayers to have a specified amount of savings income (interest from, say, savings accounts) each year free of income tax. In 2018–19, the PSA is £1,000 for people whose top rate of tax on savings income is the basic rate (20%) and £500 for people whose top rate of tax is the higher rate (40%).

Personalised financial advice Recommendations of products you should buy and/or actions you should take that are tailored to your own particular characteristics and circumstances. In most cases advice can only legally be given by a professional who is authorised by the Financial Conduct Authority.

Physical assets Assets that have an economic, commercial or exchange value and that are physical in nature (e.g. you can touch them). They include properties, equipment, furniture, cars, personal possessions.

Precautionary saving Savings that are put aside to deal with uncertain future income or unexpected expenses. An *emergency fund* (see above) is a common example.

Premium Bonds A savings product offered by the government agency, National Savings & Investments, where instead of earning interest you take part in monthly draws for prizes.

Present bias A behavioural trait where you tend to undervalue costs or benefits in the future compared with costs or benefits today, even though later you regret doing this.

Present value A way of expressing the worth of a future amount of income or cash. It is the lump sum you would need today to generate the future amount taking into account the return you could get from investing the lump sum until needed.

Private pension A pension scheme arranged by an employer or that you arrange for yourself (as opposed to a state pension which is a government scheme).

Probate (called confirmation in Scotland) Refers to the legal and financial processes involved in dealing with the property, money and possessions (called the assets) of a person who has died.

Property allowance Allows you to have up to £1,000 a year (in 2018–19) of income tax-free from your home, for example, by renting it out for a week or two or letting your driveway for parking. (Cannot be combined with rent-a-room relief.)

Psychological distance The mental gap between two things that needs to be bridged if you are to make an informed decision. For example, temporal psychological distance is the gap between the present and the future.

Reducing-balance loan A loan where you make regular payments that pay off both the interest and the amount your originally borrowed. Provided you keep up all the payments, you owe nothing by the end of the term. (A *repayment mortgage* – see below – is an example.)

Regulated financial advice Advice that falls within the remit of the Financial Conduct Authority concerning, for example, investments, loans, mortgages, insurance, and so on.

Regulated financial adviser An individual or firm who can legally give you personalised financial advice since they are regulated by the Financial Conduct Authority.

Rent-a-room relief Scheme that allows you to have up to £7,500 a year (in 2018–19) of income tax-free from renting out room(s) in your home to lodger(s).

Rent-to-own Arrangement where you buy household appliances, furniture or other items, getting to use them straight away but paying for them by regular weekly or monthly instalments. The overall cost of the items is typically much higher than if you were to buy them outright and higher than traditional *hire purchase* (see above).

Repayment mortgage A type of *mortgage* (see above) where your monthly payments pay off both the interest and amount you originally borrowed. Provided you keep up all the payments, the debt is completely cleared by the end of the mortgage term.

Residual income (recurring income) Income you continue to receive after the work that originally generated it is done.

Salary sacrifice Arrangement where you permanently give up some of your pay in return for receiving benefits in kind instead. Usually done because fringe benefits are taxed more lightly than pay.

Saving The act of setting aside some of your income today so that you can spend (or use it in some other way) later on.

Savings A stock of money that you've accumulated (which may be in the form of cash, savings accounts or investments).

Secured loan Arrangement where you borrow money and the lender can seize an asset that you own (usually your home) and sell it to get their money back if you do not keep up the agreed loan payments.

Self-insure Where you put aside a sum of money to be used in the event of unexpected loss (as opposed to buying an insurance policy).

Shares Another name for *equities* (see above).

Short term Typically refers to a period of time of five years or less.

Sick pay Income that is paid to a worker who is unable to work due to sickness.

SMART goals Targets that are specified in enough detail so that you know exactly what you are aiming for and can measure your progress towards achieving them. The letters of 'SMART' stand for specific, measurable, attainable, realistic and time-related.

State benefits Money you can get from the government if you meet specified conditions, such as having a low income or a disability.

State pension A regular income for people who have reached at least state pension age that you qualify for by paying (or being credited with) National Insurance contributions.

State pension age The minimum age at which you can start to draw your state pension.

State pension statement A record of the amount of eventual state pension you have built up so far.

Status quo bias A behavioural trait where you tend to stick with the current situation rather than changing to something else even if you would be better off switching.

Statutory Sick Pay (SSP) A minimum amount of income paid to an employee who is off sick.

Stock Another name for *equities* (see above).

Stock market The bringing together of people who want to sell investments such as equities and bonds with those who want to buy them. Previously a physical place, but these days nearly always online.

Store card Usually a type of credit card but for purchases only at one or more specified retailers.

Student loan A loan you take out to pay for higher education. In the countries of the UK, repayments stop if your income falls below a specified level and the remaining loan is written off after a specified (but lengthy) term – as a result some experts argue it is more like a form of tax rather than a true loan.

Tax allowance A specified level of income, gain, assets or other item that is tax-free but would be taxable in the absence of the allowance.

Tax credits A type of state benefit for families with children and/or people in work who have a relatively low income.

Tax exemption Being outside the scope of one or more taxes and so tax-free – for example, there is no income tax or capital gains tax on the return from an *individual savings account* (see above).

Tax relief A reduction in your tax bill if you use your money in certain ways (for example, saving for retirement or giving to charity) or meet certain conditions (such as selling a property that has been your only or main home).

Term insurance A type of life insurance which provides cover for a fixed period of time and only pays out if the person who is insured dies within this period

Trading allowance Allows you to have up to £1,000 a year (in 2018–19) of income tax-free from a very small business, such as selling crafts at fairs or online, or giving a few music lessons. (It must be your only business and you cannot claim tax relief for any expenses.)

Trust A legal arrangement where one or more people (the trustees) are the legal owners of some assets but must use them only for the benefit of specified named people or groups of people (the beneficiaries) and in accordance with any conditions set out in the document governing the trust (the trust deed).

Unauthorised overdraft Situation where you borrow from your bank by simply spending more than you have in your current account, but without having agreed this with the bank. The charges and interest if you do this are typically much higher than for an *authorised overdraft* (see above).

Uncrystallised fund pension lump sum (UFPLS) The technical name for a lump sum that you draw from a defined-contribution scheme under the policy of 'Freedom and choice' before you are ready to start a retirement income. (A quarter of the lump sum is tax-free but the rest is taxable.)

Universal credit A type of state benefit for households on a relatively low income that is gradually replacing a number of other benefits such as tax credits, help with housing costs, and so on.

Unsecured loan Arrangement where you borrow money and, if you fail to make the agreed payments, the lender would have to take you to court to try to get their money back (in contrast to a secured loan where something you own could be sold).

Whole of life insurance A type of life insurance that provides cover for the whole life of an insured person. It has no policy expiry date, and only expires when the insured person dies.

Will A legal document that sets out how your *estate* (see above) will be passed on when you die.

Work capability assessment A test to decide whether claimants are entitled to welfare sickness benefits.

Workplace pension A pension scheme that you are put into or can join through work.

Useful contacts

British Insurance Brokers Association (BIBA)
To find insurance brokers in your area who can help you choose and find insurance
Consumer helpline: 0370 950 1790
Email: enquiries@biba.org.uk
www.biba.org.uk

Chartered Institute for Securities and Investment
To find members who can give you regulated financial advice
Email: customersupport@cisi.org
Find a financial planner: www.financialplanning.org.uk/wayfinder/find-planner
Consumer website (including find a planner): www.financialplanning.org.uk/wayfinder

Chartered Institute of Taxation
To find members who can give you tax advice
Tel: 020 7340 0550
www.tax.org.uk

Citizens Advice
For advice and help with debt and state benefits; also information and guidance on almost any topic. Look in The Phone Book under 'Citizens Advice Bureau'
www.citizensadvice.org.uk

Company car tax calculator
http://cccfcalculator.hmrc.gov.uk/CCF2.aspx

Credit reference agencies
To check your credit file and correct any errors. See separate entry for each organisation for more contact options

- Experian: www.experian.co.uk
- Equifax: www.equifax.co.uk
- TransUnion (formerly called CallCredit): www.callcredit.co.uk
- CredScope: www.credscope.com

CredScope
Smaller credit reference agency that lets you build your own credit profile including non-standard but verifiable data
Tel: 0333 012 4025
www.credscope.com

Credit union – to find one
- Ask your Human Resources department at work to find out if there is a workplace scheme
- **Find Your Credit Union:** www.findyourcreditunion.co.uk
- **Ace Credit Union Services**: www.acecus.org
- **Association of British Credit Unions Ltd (ABCUL)**: www.abcul. org
- **Scottish League of Credit Unions**: www.scottishcu.org

Debt Advice Foundation
For a free online debt advice tool
www.debtadvicefoundation.org/personal-debt-analyser

Debt advice
See separate entry for each organisation for more contact options

- **Citizens Advice**: www.citizensadvice.org.uk
- **Debt Advice Foundation** online debt advice tool: www.debtad-vicefoundation.org/personal-debt-analyser
- **Money Advice Scotland**: www.moneyadvicescotland.org.uk/find-adviser
- **National Debtline**: www.nationaldebtline.co.uk online debt advice tool: www.mymoneysteps.org
- **PayPlan**: www.payplan.com
- **StepChange**: www.stepchange.org

Experian

One of the three main UK credit reference agencies. You have a right to check your credit file on payment of a fee of £2 – this is called your statutory report

'Free' indicative credit score (you pay by sharing personal data): www.experian.co.uk

Statutory report (£2): www.experian.co.uk/contact-us/

Equifax

One of the three main UK credit reference agencies. You have a right to check your credit file on payment of a statutory fee of £2

Tel: 0845 603 6772

www.equifax.co.uk

'Free' credit report and indicative score (monthly fee after the first 30 days): www.equifax.co.uk/Products/credit/credit-score.html

Statutory report (£2): www.equifax.co.uk/Products/credit/statutory-report.html

Fair For You

A lower cost alternative to the rent-to-own way of purchasing household appliances and furniture

www.fairforyou.co.uk

Financial adviser – to find one

See separate entry for each organisation for more contact options

- **Chartered Institute of Securities and Investment** Find a financial planner: www.financialplanning.org.uk/wayfinder/find-planner
- **Money Advice Service** Retirement adviser directory: *https:// directory.moneyadviceservice.org.uk/en*
- **MyLocalAdviser**: www.mylocaladviser.co.uk
- **The Personal Finance Society** (to locate a TPFS member): www. findanadviser.org
- **Personal Investment Management and Financial Advice Association**: www.pimfa.co.uk/managing-your-money/find-a-firm/
- **Society of Later Life Advisers (SOLLA)** Find an adviser: https:// societyoflaterlifeadvisers.co.uk/Find-an-adviser
- **Unbiased**: www.unbiased.co.uk
- **Vouched for**: www.vouchedfor.co.uk

Financial Conduct Authority (FCA)
The UK's financial regulator
FCA consumer helpline: 0800 111 6768
www.fca.org.uk
Consumer information: www.fca.org.uk/consumers

Financial life planning – example
Kinder Institute: www.kinderinstitute.com/planner-search/

Financial Ombudsman Service
Free service to help you resolve a problem with a financial firm (but complain to the firm first)
Tel: 0800 0 234 567 or 0300 123 9123
www.financial-ombudsman.org.uk

Financial Services Compensation Scheme
May provide compensation when a financial firm goes out of business owing customers money
Tel: 0800 678 1100 or 020 7741 4100
Email: enquiries@fscs.org.uk
www.fscs.org.uk

Financial Services Register

To check whether a financial firm is authorised by the FCA
Financial Services Register: www.fsa.gov.uk/register/home.do

Government Gateway

To register with or use government online services, such as self-assessment for online tax returns
www.gateway.gov.uk

GOV.uk

Information about all aspects of government and government services.
www.gov.uk

- **Benefits calculators** (links to): www.gov.uk/benefits-calculators
- **HM Revenue & Customs** (have your National Insurance number to hand when you phone) General enquiries: 0300 200 3300 All contact options: www.gov.uk/government/organisations/hm-revenue-customs/contact
  www.gov.uk/government/organisations/hm-revenue-customs
- **HMRC expenses and benefits from work**: www.gov.uk/expenses-and-benefits-a-to-z
- **HMRC inheritance tax** Probate and IHT Helpline: 0300 123 1072 (calls charged at normal geographic rates); inheritance tax forms: www.gov.uk/government/collections/inheritance-tax-forms www.gov.uk/inheritance-tax
- **HMRC self-assessment**: 0300 200 3310
- **Jobcentre plus**: www.gov.uk
- **Loan shark** report one: www.gov.uk/report-loan-shark
- **The Pension Service** State pension statement: Tel: 0800 731 0175; www.gov.uk/state-pension-statement
- **The Pension Tracing Service**: Tel: 0800 731 0193; www.gov.uk/find-lost-pension
- **Tax-Free Childcare** savings scheme: www.gov.uk/help-with-childcare-costs/tax-free-childcare

Illegal money lending team
To report an illegal lender (loan shark) to the authorities
www.gov.uk/report-loan-shark

- **England**: Email *reportaloanshark@stoploansharks.gov.uk;* Tel: 0300 555 2222; Text: 07860 022 116
- **Wales**: Email *imlu@cardiff.gov.uk;* Tel: 0300 123 3311; Text: 07772 608 931
- **Scotland**: www.tsscot.co.uk/report; Tel: 0800 074 0878
- **Northern Ireland**: www.consumerline.org; Tel: 0300 123 6262

Online investment guidance – some examples
- Nutmeg: www.nutmeg.com
- Scaleable Capital: https://uk.scalable.capital/investment-universe
- Moola: https://moo.la
- Wealthify: www.wealthify.com

Jobcentre Plus
To claim state benefits
For local office, look in *The Phone Book* under 'Jobcentre Plus' or 'Social security'.
www.gov.uk

Local council
To claim some state benefits, such as housing benefit and help paying council tax. Look in The Phone Book under 'Councils' or the relevant council's name
www.gov.uk/find-your-local-council

Money Advice Scotland
To find debt advice if you live in Scotland
Helpline: 0800 731 4722
www.moneyadvicescotland.org.uk/find-adviser

Money Advice Service (MAS)

For information and guidance on any aspect of your personal finances. From January 2019, MAS is due to be replaced by a new single public guidance body – once this happens, the MAS website should give new contact details

Money advice line: 0800 138 7777 or (Welsh) 0800 138 0555

Email: enquiries@moneyadviceservice.org.uk

www.moneyadviceservice.org.uk

Annuity comparison website: www.moneyadviceservice.org.uk/en/tools/annuities

Healthcheck tool: www.moneyadviceservice.org.uk/en/tools/health-check

Retirement adviser directory: https://directory.moneyadviceservice.org.uk/en

Money therapy – some examples
- Financial Coaching: https://financial-coaching.co.uk/
- Money Coaching Institute: moneycoachinginstitute.com

Mortgage adviser
- www.unbiased.co.uk
- www.mylocaladviser.co.uk

MyLocalAdviser

To find an adviser on any aspect of personal finance

www.mylocaladviser.co.uk

National Debtline

For advice and help with debt problems

Tel: 0808 808 4000 (freephone)

www.nationaldebtline.co.uk

Online debt advice tool: https://www.mymoneysteps.org/

National Savings & Investments (NS&I)

For information about NS&I products and to buy and manage them online
Tel: 0808 500 7007
www.nsandi.com

NHS Choices

For directories of services that can help with addiction problems (which can often lead to debt problems)
www.nhs.uk/live-well/healthy-body/addiction-what-is-it/

Occupational pension schemes

See scheme handbook, recent benefit statement, annual report or noticeboard at work for contact details of pension scheme adminis-trator or trustees. Alternatively, contact your HR department

The Open University

For free courses about money and personal finance
OpenLearn: www.open.edu/openlearn/
FutureLearn: www.futurelearn.com
Managing My Money: www.open.edu/openlearn/money-manage-ment/managing-my-money/content-section-overview?active-tab=description-tab
Managing My Money for Young Adults: www.open.edu/openlearn/money-business/personal-finance/managing-my-money-young-adults/content-section-overview?active-tab=description-tab
Managing My Investments: www.open.edu/openlearn/money-man-agement/managing-my-investments/content-section-overview?active-tab=description-tab

PayPlan

For advice and help with debt problems
Tel: 0808 278 6944
www.payplan.com

Pension Protection Fund (PPF)

For information about what happens if your employer's pension scheme fails. Contact with the PPF will normally be through your pension scheme administrators at work
Tel: 0345 600 2541
Email: information@ppf.gsi.gov.uk
www.pensionprotectionfund.org.uk

The Pension Service

For information about, and to claim, your state pension. For your local office, look in The Phone Book under 'The Pension Service' or 'Social security'
State pension statement, Tel: 0800 731 0175
www.gov.uk/state-pension-statement
www.gov.uk

Pension Tracing Service

A free government service to find lost pensions. (Do not confuse with commercial websites that use similar names but charge you)
The Pension Service 9
Mail Handling Site A
Wolverhampton WV98 1LU
Tel: 0800 731 0193
www.gov.uk/find-lost-pension

Pension Wise

Free government guidance for the over-50s about defined-contribution pensions, including the 'freedom and choice' options from age 55. From January 2019, Pension Wise is due to be replaced by a new single public guidance body – once this happens, the Pension Wise website should give new contact details
www.pensionwise.gov.uk/en
Book a phone or face-to-face appointment: www.pensionwise.gov.uk/en/appointments

The Pensions Advisory Service (TPAS)

For information and guidance about any aspect of pensions. From January 2019, TPAS is due to be replaced by a new single public guidance body – once this happens, the TPAS website should give new contact details

Tel: 0800 011 3797 or (self-employed) 0345 602 7021
www.pensionsadvisoryservice.org.uk
Annuity Planner: www.pensionsadvisoryservice.org.uk/my-pension/online-tools

Pensions Ombudsman

Free service to help you resolve complaints about workplace pensions. (You should first raise the matter with your scheme)

Tel: 0800 917 4487
Email: enquiries@pensions-ombudsman.org.uk
www.pensions-ombudsman.org.uk

The Pensions Regulator

Regulates workplace pension schemes

www.thepensionsregulator.gov.uk
Report a concern (whistleblowers) Tel: 0345 600 7060
Email: wb@tpr.gov.uk
Who can help you: www.thepensionsregulator.gov.uk/individuals.aspx

The Personal Finance Society

To find members who can give you regulated financial advice
To locate a TPFS member: www.findanadviser.org

Personal Investment Management and Financial Advice Association (formerly known as the Wealth Management Association)

To find members who can give you regulated financial advice and/or manage your investments for you

Tel: 020 7448 7100
Email: info@pimfa.co.uk
www.pimfa.co.uk/managing-your-money/find-a-firm/

Price comparison websites – some examples
To help you find savings, loans, insurance and other financial products

- **Compare the Market**: www.comparethemarket.com
- **Moneyfacts**: www.moneyfacts.co.uk
- **Moneysupermarket**: www.moneysupermarket.com
- **uSwitch**: www.uswitch.com

Revenue Scotland
The tax authority that deals with Scottish income tax and other taxes devolved to the Scotland Parliament
PO Box 24068
Victoria Quay
Edinburgh EH6 9BR
Tel: 03000 300 310
www.revenue.scot

Social Security and Child Support Appeals Tribunal
Handles appeals if you have been denied state benefits you believe you are entitled to. Apply for an appeal through your usual Pension Service or Jobcentre Plus office. See DWP leaflet GL24 If you think our decision is wrong
www.gov.uk/social-security-child-support-tribunal

Society of Later Life Advisers (SOLLA)
To find a member who can give regulated financial advice particularly on pensions, retirement and other later life matters
Tel: 0333 202 0454
Email: admin@societyoflaterlifeadvisers.co.uk
https://societyoflaterlifeadvisers.co.uk/
Find an adviser: https://societyoflaterlifeadvisers.co.uk/Find-an-adviser

Society of Trust and Estate Practitioners (STEP)
To find a solicitor or financial adviser who specialises in estate planning, inheritance tax and setting up and managing trusts

Tel: 020 3752 3700
Email: step@step.org
www.step.org
Member directory: www.step.org/member-directory

StepChange
For advice and help with problem debts
Tel: 0800 138 1111
www.stepchange.org
Online debt tool: www.stepchange.org/Debtremedy.aspx

Tax adjudicator
Deals with complaints about HMRC mismanagement of your tax affairs. You must take your complaint first to HMRC
PO Box 10280
Nottingham NG2 9PF
Tel: 0300 057 1111
www.adjudicatorsoffice.gov.uk

Tax advisers – to find one
See separate entry for each organisation for more contact options

- **Chartered Institute of Taxation**: www.tax.org.uk
- **Society of Trust and Estate Practitioners (STEP)** Member directory: www.step.org/member-directory
- **TaxAid** (free advice for people on a low income): www.taxaid.org.uk
- **Tax Help for Older People (TOP)** (free advice for older people on a low income): www.taxvol.org.uk

TaxAid
Free advice for people who are on a low income and cannot afford to pay for tax advice
Tel: 0345 120 3779
www.taxaid.org.uk

Tax-Free Childcare
A government scheme that helps you save to pay for the cost of childcare
www.gov.uk/help-with-childcare-costs/tax-free-childcare

Tax Help for Older People (TOP)
Free advice for older people who are on a low income and cannot afford to pay for tax advice
Tel: 0845 601 3321 or 01308 488 066
www.taxvol.org.uk

Tax tribunal
For appeals against a tax assessment or penalty. You must first have taken this up with HMRC
First-tier Tribunal (Tax Chamber)
PO Box 16972
Birmingham B16 6TZ
Tel: 0300 123 1024
Email: taxappeals@hmcts.gsi.gov.uk
www.gov.uk/courts-tribunals/first-tier-tribunal-tax

TransUnion (formerly called CallCredit)
One of the three main UK credit reference agencies. You have a right to check your credit file on payment of a fee of £2 – this is called your statutory report
Tel: 0330 024 7574
www.callcredit.co.uk
Noddle offers reports and an indicative credit score (although 'free' in the sense that there are no money charges, you pay by agreeing to share your personal data with other firms): www.callcredit.co.uk/consumer-solutions/your-credit-report/free-credit-report
Statutory report (£2): www.callcreditstatreport.co.uk

Unbiased
For a list of financial advisers or mortgage advisers in your area
www.unbiased.co.uk

Vouched for
To find a financial or legal expert
www.vouchedfor.co.uk

Welsh Revenue Authority
The tax authority that deals with taxes devolved to the Welsh Assembly
PO Box 10
Pontypridd CF37 9EH
Tel: 0300 025 4000
https://beta.gov.wales/welsh-revenue-authority

Index

Note: italics indicate figures; bold indicates tables.